WAINWRIGHT
REVEALED

by Richard Else

First published 2017 by Mountain Media Productions Ltd

Mountain Media Productions Ltd
Old Glen Road
Newtonmore
Inverness–shire PH20 1EB

www.mountain–media.co.uk

©Mountain Media 2017

Text by Richard Else. Foreword by Eric Robson.

Design and layout by Tide Graphic Design Consultants Ltd.

Set in 11pt Athelas.

Printed by Bell & Bain, Glasgow.

ISBN– 978–0–9562–9574–3

Contact details, accommodation and travel information are believed to correct at the time of going to press.

PAGE 1 – Ben Loyal seen from Lochan Hakel. Wainwright first visited the far north of Scotland during his annual holidays, travelling entirely by train and bus.

PAGE 3 – AW & presenter Eric Robson above Robin Hood's Bay after completing the Coast to Coast walk.

PAGE 4 – Wainwright's first brief letter to the author.

WAINWRIGHT
REVEALED

by Richard Else

38 Kendal Green, KENDAL, Cumbria,
11th May 1982

Dear Mr Else,

Thankyou for your letter of the 6th., about which I had been forewarned!

As you have been informed, I would not consider either an interview or an appearance on TV, this sort of publicity not being my cup of tea at all, but you may quote from my books or show my drawings to any extent you wish. If you are wanting autobiographical details, you will find all I am prepared to divulge in my book titled 'Fellwanderer'.

I wish you well if you decide to go ahead with the idea. The programme you have in mind should meet with the approval of the many fellwalkers in your area.

Yours sincerely,

AWainwright

Contents

Filming in the Lakes with Eric Robson, camera person John Warwick, assistant Paul Otter and sound recordist John G Pearson.

Foreword

When Richard first mentioned this book to me and outlined the themes he hoped to address in it, I confess that I didn't think he'd be able to carry it off. Surely we only ever scratched the surface of Alfred Wainwright's complex character? Even after all the months of filming together, the passions that drove him remained locked in his private, silent world.

Yes, we made him into an unlikely television star but it was on his terms. Yes, he grew to trust us more as series followed series but to the end, if I asked him a question that threatened to stray over the boundaries he'd set, all I'd get was a long sigh and a cloud of tobacco smoke. Against that background Richard had surely set himself an impossible task.

I was wrong. Richard has produced a book that's entertaining and knowledgeable in equal measure. I should never have doubted him. It was, after all, the young Mr Else who persuaded AW to sup with the devil in the first place and against his better judgement agree to work with us television people. It was Richard who persuaded him that being interviewed by this Robson chap wasn't a stepping stone to purgatory and that talking about how and why he produced his Pictorial guides wouldn't in some mysterious way diminish them.

The book also reminded me that however cantankerous Wainwright could be at times, he was also great company. He had a Sahara–dry sense of humour and a philosophical and poetic turn of phrase sadly lacking in the work of so many guidebook writers. Richard's fondness for and knowledge of Wainwright have created a readable and fascinating new portrait of a charming, gentle and obsessive man.

There's also the odd giggle at the expense of a certain reporter who had the tricky job of trying to extract more than a dozen words a day from his unwilling interviewee. But of course that's what reporters are there for.

Eric Robson
Wainwright's walking companion and Chair, *Gardeners Question Time*, Radio 4

Introduction

This book has involved revisiting many of the places I shared with AW in the 1980s, some of which, like the Little Chef at Ings, north of Kendal, have been consigned to history. Sometimes the changes have been so profound it feels as if I'm visiting a foreign land. That applies not simply to the townships and villages, but to the fells themselves. Equally, other places have survived with little alteration.

Looking at many of the photographs from that time takes me back to events and places that are still fresh in the memory. There is Ben Hope, the most northerly of Scotland's Munros, in the hazy sunshine of a late spring afternoon. Here Wainwright wanted to capture not simply the remoteness of that glen (where the grass was growing in the middle of the single track road), but also to share the uncertain history of the broch that stands sentinel in Strath More. Or there is Loch Muick with a bite in the early autumn wind and AW still trying to make out the detail on his old Bartholomew map – detail rendered opaque by failing eyesight that was beyond repair. More than any of these memorable days is Wainwright's final long walk. Nowhere could be more appropriate that an ascent of Haystacks, on a day when every step was wrung from the wind and driving rain. Yet it is not only the landscapes that are imprinted on my mind, it is what they meant to AW. I was intrigued by how these elemental, inanimate forces shaped his life, and why their impact was infinitely more significant than any single human influence. When we were filming much of this was caught on camera, but it wasn't just what he said – a facial expression, a hand movement or a long hard stare at the lens could be equally revealing.

There is a specific date to the start of my relationship with AW and his wife, Betty. It is a typewritten letter from AW himself and exactly fitted the inside page of an Animal Rescue Cumbria notelet. So exactly did it fit the page, that I'm sure he must have carefully formulated the wording before committing it to print. There is also a formality to it. Later on, his letters to me were handwritten.

From that day in 1982, AW and I travelled approximately 5,000 miles together. We explored his beloved Lakeland; roamed the solitary upland of the Howgill Fells; tramped part of the Pennine Way and celebrated Wainwright's own creation – the Coast to Coast walk. The other great high point for me was our Scottish journeys.

The last light fades behind the summit of Blencathra. This mountain was a favourite hill of Wainwright's. I had hoped to include the northern fells in our first series and looked at various places we might film. In the end the plan was abandoned once AW had agreed to return to Haystacks.

For a year and more we explored this most magical of landscapes. Those journeys finally took us back to AW's home town of Blackburn and the memories locked within its industrial past.

There were many poignant moments, especially when it became clear that the decline in his health was not just confined to his eyesight. There were times when he and Betty seemed to set themselves against the world, anxious over a range of perceived problems. Sometimes I worried about how much this had been accelerated by the television programmes which had seen his profile grow from a much admired, yet niche, author to a national institution and, much as he would have disliked the word, a celebrity.

One final comment is necessary: I did not set out to write a controversial book but am aware that to many people Wainwright is viewed as a hero who can do little, if any, wrong. I believe that does him and his work no justice. I feel it would not gain his approval. This book is about an extraordinary, talented individual; about someone compelled by forces he may not himself have fully understood; and about someone whose best works can genuinely be judged as literary masterpieces.

A note on the text

In almost all cases I have abbreviated Wainwright's seven–volume *Pictorial Guide to the Lakeland Fells* to simply the *Guide* – singular, rather than plural. This seems more accurate to me as AW conceived of it as a single work and it is a description he used.

When I refer to other works I have included them within the text, rather than placing them at the end. This seems more natural and I hope it does not impede the flow of the text. I have tried to avoid unnecessary duplication about AW's life and his works, especially in view of Hunter Davies' *Wainwright – The Biography* (with its useful bibliography) and *The Wainwright Letters*. I have also assumed that readers will want to refer to AW's original works, to see my comments in a wider context. All these books are now published by Frances Lincoln.

Richard Else

Newtonmore, July 2017.

Wainwright at his happiest. This picture was taken in the upper reaches of Gleann Lichd, near the end of a wonderful day's filming. Like so many places we visited together, Wainwright had not expected to be here again.

1. In the beginning

In the beginning. A spell of bad weather seen from the summit of Haystacks. When making the films I would often spend a night here, camping not by Innominate Tarn but on a small patch of ground near the summit. AW could never really understand why I enjoyed lightweight backpacking and was unconvinced when I said I had slept soundly. This book began with another night on the summit, although I had to make a number of visits before suitable weather allowed me to get the photographs I wanted.

The beginning of my fascination with Wainwright's work – specifically the *Guide* – can be traced back to an exact moment in time. It was a snow-covered night between Christmas and New Year 1976 and with the help of some rudimentary snow chains my loved but unreliable Hillman Imp was making slow, steady progress up a hill that leads south-west from the small village of Helton, a few miles south from Penrith, onto Askham Fell. I parked the car at the start of the fell and walked back with my partner Meg through spindrift and deepening snow to one of the last cottages. In a house that dated back to the 17th century her cousins, Alan and Sarah, had made their new home.

As the evening wore on, Alan went to the bookshelf and handed me a small volume. He said casually, 'Have you seen this?' It would be wonderful if I could say that as soon as I saw *The Far Eastern Fells*, the second volume of *AW's Guide*, I instantly had a moment of revelation. But it isn't true and, in fact, I was struggling to make sense of it. I had heard of Wainwright some years earlier on a school fieldwork trip to the Lakes. I recall seeing his final volume, *The Western Fells*, which had been published only four years previous to that visit, in a Keswick bookshop window, but at that time I was more interested in the romantic poets. I could have bought the Wainwright volume but opted instead for a selected edition of Wordsworth. Today I would buy both.

Sitting in the thick-walled cottage, the noise of the storm outside was reduced to a quiet muffle. The fire was a glow of embers as I began to look through *The Far Eastern Fells*. Alan, who had a well-used early edition with the rounded corners, told me that the man who had written and illustrated it was both a local legend and a recluse.

When Wainwright wrote his Guide to the Northern Fells he met with few other walkers. When I first started exploring these hills little had changed from AW's original visits. Even today you can have a popular spot like Bowscale Tarn to yourself by arriving early or lingering late.

After some difficulty, I worked out that Arthur's Pike was the nearest hill to feature in the book, so I began there. I started with the map in this chapter and, attempting to get a bigger picture of the surrounding land, was soon turning the pages, off to the Loadpot Hill chapter then onto Wether Hill, trying to understand how all these small maps interlinked. By accident, on page 8 of the Loadpot Hill chapter, I discovered that the cottage I was sitting in appeared on the map, drawn by AW's distinctive hand.

Yet I was still mystified by a book that didn't seem at all intuitive. To find what lay on the other side of Ullswater I had to find Wainwright's first book – *The Eastern Fells* – and look up Gowbarrow Fell. To try to piece this part of Lakeland together and get an overview of an area was hard work. There was much I liked about the books – the precise handwriting; illustrations that were a lesson in economy but nonetheless gave evocative images of the summits, crags, fellsides and valleys; the maps were a work of art, and the final section, *Some Personal Notes in Conclusion,* was by turn witty, moving and lyrical. Most of all, it gave some insight into a highly unusual and, I guessed, solitary individual. And that, for the moment, was that. At the end of our visit I handed the book back and we headed south to the folds of Derbyshire's White Peak.

Five years later, I had exchanged a job in local radio for one in television and reluctantly left an old house a few miles from Matlock, for one in the suburbs of Cardiff. I had lived in Wales before and had a great affection for it. The Brecon Beacons weren't far away; the wild, sparsely populated spaces of mid-Wales opened out just beyond them and that little England beyond Wales, Pembrokeshire, was within striking distance. All in all, not bad but with one massive drawback – working on the nightly news programme in Wales was, at that time, sheer hell. My services were not required in the morning by a programme editor who saw any kind of collaboration as a threat to his authority and as an attempt to sabotage his masterpiece. I am still convinced it served as a template for *Drop the Dead Donkey.* But perhaps all newsrooms are like that. There was one consolation. Thirty and more years ago many BBC premises had their own library, complete with librarian, and it was in that quiet sanctuary – away from the orchestrated chaos of the newsroom – that I spent a couple of hours each day thinking of how it might be possible to escape. Having made a mistake once, I wanted to be sure about my next move.

That's when I began to think seriously about those seven volumes Wainwright had written. I started by exploring the structure of each book and how the various elements fitted together. Some months later I was still at the task and was now conducting a forensic examination of each book and making copious notes. I remember wanting to try to understand them in the way their author did, to understand his motivation and the perseverance required for such an undertaking. I knew little about A.Wainwright but I had a section in my notes listing his qualities: *diligence, accuracy, determination, endurance, sacrifice, planned like a military campaign* were there along with many others. I pored over the introduction, the individual sections describing each fell and summit and read and re-read those *Personal Notes in Conclusion*.

AW and Betty photographed when I was on holiday with them in the west of Scotland. Here Wainwright was relaxed and eager to share this part of Scotland with me. I also witnessed how much AW relied on Betty as a wife, chauffeur, manager and companion. Without Betty I suspect there would have been no films and Wainwright might have become more reclusive and isolated.

I laid out the relevant Ordnance Survey maps and thought about how, using these together with his own personal explorations year after year, Wainwright had formulated his grand plan. I also began to think about their historical context: framing works that began in the shadow of post-war austerity and were completed as the 'swinging sixties' ushered in a new mood and culture. People had spoken to me about the books as walking guides to the fells and although you can use them in that way, I didn't share that view. To me, then and now, they were works of significant literary merit, works that could sit alongside what, in the early 1980s, was a neglected genre of guidebook and outdoor writing.

As a young programme maker, I became intrigued by the *Guide* and the man behind it. In a phrase, I was hooked.

A traditional barn at Watendlath. Wainwright was fascinated by all aspects of Lakeland. Although he loved the high tops, he was equally interested in its traditions, culture, history and those people who shaped what we see today.

If, at its best, life is a series of happy coincidences, my luck was about to change dramatically. A post as a television features producer was advertised at BBC Newcastle and even more importantly, investigation revealed that the head of department was everything my current boss wasn't. He was said to be hugely experienced, incredibly supportive, exceptionally well read and someone who cared passionately about his patch of north-east England and the northern part of Cumbria. I had already come across his name but didn't, at that time, know how important he would be. He is John Mapplebeck and now, in his eighties, he is still the same wonderful polymath he was in the 1980s. It is no exaggeration to say that without him Wainwright would never have made it onto the small screen.

When I caught the overnight sleeper to Newcastle for an interview, it was so cold the water in the ancient carriage was frozen solid. As I walked up to the BBC that day I had two objectives – this was the one job I really wanted and there was one film more than any other I was determined to make. My chances of success? At the most optimistic, a very long shot – I lacked a lot of local knowledge, I was pretty inexperienced and, as final disincentive, there would almost certainly be someone who was doing the job already.

Anyone other than John Mapplebeck would not have taken me on. It was John's willingness to take a chance that led me, Meg, two small children, a cross bearded collie and an old caravan to the rolling and sparsely inhabited landscape of Northumberland.

My plan was a simple one that I'd outlined at my interview, or as the BBC like to call it, 'board'. I said, with a confidence belying my inner feelings, that it should be possible to make a programme about Wainwright. But I also knew that AW would not agree to appear. I didn't think it necessary to point this out to those on the other side of the table. In fact, by this time I knew that a number of well-known television figures had tried to make a programme about the reclusive, pipe-smoking author from Kendal. Others had attempted interviews, radio programmes or book projects. All had failed. I may have forgotten to mention this at my interview.

The reason why those approaches had been unsuccessful seemed clear to me – unlike many authors who actively crave publicity, AW was the opposite, someone who had no apparent interest in appearing on either radio or television. This reluctance translated in a very simple way as far as the mainstream media were concerned – without the man himself, there could be no programme. Only someone with the vision of John Mapplebeck could see what to me was obvious: surely the best way to make a film about such a figure was to accept that he would almost certainly be absent. We could, therefore, make the film with the understanding that we did not need the star. I always remember putting a sheet of paper into my typewriter and beginning to write the treatment. *Title: Wainwright.* A simple one-word title would do.

It was a decision I believe very few commissioning editors would be brave enough to make. On that precarious basis I started work from a small shared office in a rundown 1930s building in Newcastle, but within a few weeks I was out on the fellside by day and reading by night.

2. Just this once

Just this once. High Street and Kidsty Pike (far right) seen from the old Corpse Road above Haweswater reservoir. When we filmed here I was surprised by AW's comments. I expected the reservoir would spoil his early memory of this fine landscape, but he was still enthusiastic about the surrounding summits, the long ridge of High Street and the many small details that are often overlooked by walkers heading for the summits.

L iving in a caravan that had seen much better days is not as romantic as it might sound. Any hot water had to be boiled in a kettle, the heating was primitive and potentially dangerous, the lights ran on gas and had fragile mantles, cooking had to be planned to make maximum use of two rings and a grill and the chemical toilet was far removed from the efficient ones in use today. When we could receive television, it was a black and white image on a small screen. But the view outside the windows of the rolling Northumberland landscape at least made up for the deficiencies inside.

Each night for eleven weeks the Falklands war rumbled on in the background. But there was one bonus – with the children in bed, I had plenty of time to read.

I began a list of themes that recurred throughout the books, I noted which places had most inspired AW and I began to form a view about the man. Tucked away in the books there is not only much biographical information but also many insights into his psychological make-up.

In tandem with this, I started to think about the people in Lakeland who might be able to speak knowledgeably about Wainwright. I knew it would not be a long list and I wanted only those would could offer a genuine insight into the man. Percy Duff was already working in the Kendal Borough Treasurer's office when AW arrived from Blackburn and, apart from a period of war service, had worked with him until AW's retirement. Then there was the noted author, *Guardian* columnist and mountaineer, Harry Griffin who lived not far away on the other side of the Windermere road. Geoffrey Berry was Chair of the Friends of the Lake District while Sid Cross, the well-known former landlord of the Old Dungeon Ghyll in Langdale, could put the *Guide* in a wider context.

Wainwright at home in Kendal Green looking at a paste-up he had done for one of his Michael Joseph books. Behind him are some of the outdoor books he owned, including works by F S Smythe, and others relating to places in Europe and beyond that he would never visit. I was impressed by his knowledge of contemporary mountaineering events and we often spoke about new achievements in the Alps and Himalayas.

But there was one thing I needed to do first – write to Wainwright himself. Partly there was an element of politeness in this but there was also an ulterior motive: I needed his permission to use quotations and illustrations from the books. I also played what I thought was my master card, saying that I fully understood that he would not wish to take part in any programme and that I wanted to make the film because of my personal admiration for what he had done. A few days later a typed envelope with a Kendal postmark arrived on my desk. I looked at it for a while, felt its weight in my hands and then carefully opened it. Inside was one of the cards produced to raise funds for the cause closest to AW's heart, Animal Rescue Cumbria. And there, neatly typed, were five sentences. I read them a number of times and then punched the air. Success. Of course, on that day in May 1982, I had no inkling of what would follow.

During the course of that day I re-read the note many times, trying to discover if anything extra could be gleaned from its contents. It appeared straightforward:

> *Dear Mr Else,*
>
> *Thank you for your letter of the 6th, about which I had been forewarned!*
>
> *As you have been informed, I would not consider either an interview or an appearance on TV, this sort of publicity not being my cup of tea at all, but you may quote from my books or show my drawings to any extent you wish. If you are wanting autobiographical details, you will find all I am prepared to divulge in my book titled 'Fellwanderer'.*
>
> *I wish you well if you decide to go ahead with the idea. The programme you have in mind should meet with the approval of the many fellwalkers in your area.*
>
> *Yours sincerely,*
>
> *A. Wainwright.*

I had managed to get the all-important permission to quote from the books and to show the work. Without such permission the project would have been grounded indefinitely. Now it had been given a green light.

A meeting of two pipes. David Bean (left) was a keen outdoors man and the presenter of our original film with Wainwright. With him, sporting a checked mountaineering shirt, was the writer and fellow Kendal resident Harry Griffin. He was one of the few people to know AW and, in his own distinctive way, another Lake District institution.

We would have one week to make our 30-minute film and fitting everything into that schedule required detailed preparation. The presenter was a figure well-known in the north-east at that time, David Bean. Although born and brought up in London, David had lived in the region for many years, earning a living as a writer and also the presenter of a successful television series shown locally, *Bean's Boots*. David lived just south of Hadrian's Wall near Haltwhistle and was rooted in the outdoors and local history. He was inquisitive by nature and, like Wainwright, his clothes had a lived-in look. I thought he would get on well with our interviewees.

Contacting them was a steep learning curve. My first call was to Harry Griffin and the conversation lasted only a couple of minutes. The phone was answered with a military style, 'Griffin here'. I had barely managed to outline why I was calling, when I was cut short with, 'I'll see you a week on Thursday at 11.00am. Goodbye'. And with that the receiver was put down. Percy Duff was more chatty and keen to help.

He provided a lot of information about AW that was vital for our film. More importantly Percy was key in advocating it to his old boss. Another keen supporter was Andrew Nichol, the printing manager at the *Westmorland Gazette*. He was responsible for overseeing an author who kept their presses running virtually full-time. Crucially, both met with Wainwright on a regular basis and I knew they would brief him about our film. Also appearing in this documentary portrait were Harry Firth, the former printing manager of the *Westmorland Gazette*, and head printer Eric Teby, the man tasked with the full-time occupation of keeping all AW's work available.

It was the height of summer when we started filming. The Lakeland roads were crowded and the towns and valleys full of tourists, so progress was slow. After two days we had the first interviews and some excellent shots of Lakeland. So far, so good. We had returned to the hotel when I got a phone call from Andrew Nichol. His message was simple and to the point: 'AW would like to see you. He doesn't like the idea of everyone talking about him and not having a chance to say anything. So I'd bring the film crew with you. 10.00am, Kendal Green. Best of luck…'

'You've got a scoop, young man.' Those were the first words AW spoke to me. Thinking that honesty was the best answer, my reply was equally brief, 'Yes, I have. Thank you.'

Wainwright had clearly thought very carefully about this interview. It was, he said, the first and last he would give on television. David Bean and I had prepared a series of questions. Separately, AW had also rehearsed a series of different answers. My immediate task was to get the two to work in tandem, but there was another potential obstacle to be overcome. Filming the interview on a seat by the side of the house was clearly the best place. But then our guest surprised us all by announcing: 'What will happen is this… The camera will start on a close-up of my chimney with some smoke coming out… just like you see on the westerns. It will move dramatically down to find a solitary figure… me… here… just like John Wayne… and then I will say….' By now we were trying hard not to laugh. Wainwright was absolutely clear about the manner in which he wanted to make his first television entrance. Most camera people would have found this difficult and probably said that if he kept to his job, they would keep to theirs. Fortunately, John Warwick was a fine arts graduate and someone who revelled in these surreal moments. Peering round from the back of his bulky 16mm camera, he beamed at AW and said, 'Thank you. That'll do just fine...'

The programme was first broadcast in the North East and Cumbria in late 1982 and ensured that my sojourn in a leaking caravan became a more permanent one in the hills of the high Pennines. We had always planned that the programme would be shown across the whole BBC Network and so at exactly 7.05pm on Tuesday 3rd May 1983, this most reluctant of television stars made his first appearance throughout the United Kingdom.

The *Radio Times* billing simply read:

Wainwright

Wainwright's Guide to the Lakeland Fells is well known to all those who love the Lakes. Painstakingly written by hand over 13 years, they made the author a legend in his own lifetime; but Wainwright himself has always avoided publicity, remaining a totally private man... In tonight's programme A. Wainwright gives his first interview and reflects on the epic work he began 30 years ago.

The programme billing in *Radio Times* was understated. But after years of anonymity, Wainwright made his television debut in style. He appeared assured and confident and there was an unmistakable twinkle in his eye as he spoke about how he had always avoided being recognised on the fells. I was unaware of it at the time, but a process had started that would soon become unstoppable. Before long there would be a series of coffee table books published by Michael Joseph, countless offers to undertake other work and AW's appearance on *Desert Island Discs*.

Although as we left that day and said our goodbyes, Wainwright looked at me and said, 'It's just this once, you understand...'

Wainwright was proud of his Coast to Coast walk and delighted to revisit much of it during our filming. The North York Moors may lack some of Lakeland's obvious drama, but in its place they provide a landscape that is wild, remote and with a fascinating history. AW enjoyed his time at Bloworth Crossing on the old Rosedale railway and, in its day, possibly the most remote level crossing in Britain.

Where do the gooseberries come from?

The Little Chef at Ings near Staveley, a short drive north-west of Kendal, was a favourite haunt of AW's and somewhere we spent many happy hours. (The love affair, incidentally, was not reciprocated. The then owners refused us permission to film and, in doing so, forfeited a huge amount of free publicity.) We never went anywhere else for lunch, in spite of me suggesting other places that I knew would appeal to AW. Likewise we never needed to look at the menu, for in all our meals there, our choice was always the same – fish and chips, pancakes and tea for AW. I was fascinated that Wainwright never thought about changing his order. It was fixed as the moon orbiting the earth and an anchor that assured him all was well in a changing world. On one occasion we were talking about our forthcoming filming in Scotland when Wainwright suddenly stopped me mid-sentence 'Now, Richard, this is really important...', he began, before pausing for a moment. I always tried to anticipate what the question might be and have an answer at least half prepared. In those few seconds, I thought about our previous conversation and made a guess at what would be coming. It would be something about permission to film on private land, or how far up a glen we might get my Land Rover or possibly about travel time from the hotel to our location and back again. I could reassure him on all three points. 'Richard, this is important', said AW with renewed emphasis. Alright, here we go, I thought.

> *'Gooseberries', said AW and looked sternly at me. Gooseberries? Why would gooseberries be relevant to our filming in the far north of Scotland? I couldn't recall seeing any in Sutherland, but then I hadn't been looking for them. Anyway why gooseberries, not raspberries or strawberries or any other fruit for that matter? AW was about to continue.*
> *'Gooseberries. Where do the gooseberries come from? The gooseberries for the pancakes? You never see them delivered? How do they get the gooseberries here? Do they come in the middle of the night?' At which point I had a vision of Little Chef staff smuggling them in under cover of darkness on a moonless night. 'I've no idea, AW'. 'Well, can you find out then? I'd like to know.' Another item was added to the 'to do' list.*

I am also sure he would have been nonplussed when the place finally closed and would have struggled to find a suitable alternative that suited his need for a fixed menu and portions that never varied.

3. The reluctant star

The reluctant star. Although the smallest of the Yorkshire three peaks, Pen-y-ghent forms a unmistakable outline, whether seen from Horton in Ribblesdale or, as here, from the south. AW's ascent for our first film together marked the real beginning of our relationship and the birth of one of television's most unlikely stars.

When the first programme was completed and broadcast I thought my job had been accomplished. I had set myself a simple goal – to make a film celebrating AW's life and work and that had been achieved. It only gradually occurred to me that it might be possible to make other films with him.

I have always been attracted to reclusive personalities and, in spite of the vast difference in our ages, AW and I shared a common heritage. I was very close to my grandparents who lived in a pit village not dissimilar, in its industrial foundations, to Wainwright's Blackburn. As I young child, I saw how poor they were and the hard life they endured. When AW's *Western Fells* was published they still had an outside toilet, no bathroom or hot water and their village had been decimated by one of the biggest post-war mining accidents. When AW talked about his background – the early morning clogs on the street outside and the inability to pay the weekly rent – I could continue the conversation, not out of sympathy, but from personal experience. I was also seeing a different side of AW, one that was more mischievous but had significant undercurrents. One morning Percy Duff came in and told Wainwright he had some sad news. One of their colleagues from the Treasurers Department had died after a nasty illness. Wainwright listened attentively, asked for the details and for his condolences to be passed on. But no sooner was Percy out of the door than AW turned to me and said, 'There you are Richard... Another non-smoker dead'. Betty was not amused. Meanwhile AW relit his pipe and began to talk about some more filming.

The fascinating geology of Pen-y-ghent - millstone grit on a base layer of limestone - and the superb views made this a favourite hill for AW.
He was also keen to show us the purple saxifrage that drapes the limestone cliffs, but unfortunately it was past its best when we came to film.

I did, however, have misgivings. I was all too aware that there is an enormous difference between featuring someone in a single programme and the bigger prospect of building a whole series around them. Our original film had been sufficiently successful that persuading BBC2 executives to take a series of programmes was not too difficult. I was, however, wrestling with a far bigger question – what would they look like and how could I make them work?

Left to make a decision by himself, Wainwright would almost certainly not have agreed to appear on television again. During our filmed interview in Kendal Green that marked his television debut, he had been in charge. When we met to discuss a possible series, I could see him trying to grapple with a number of practical problems, none of which related to his own performance. Who would feed the cats if he and Betty were away overnight? Would he be back in time for *Coronation Street*? Would it be possible to get the football results on Saturday? Where were the nearest fish and chip shops? Did I have a map showing all the Little Chefs?

In the past three (now almost four) decades I have worked with a variety of television personalities from newcomers to the highly experienced. But they all have one thing in common. None of them asked the questions that preoccupied AW. I remember one Friday morning in the living room at Kendal Green. When it seemed as if the difficulties might be insurmountable, Betty intervened. As always, she had been following the conversation closely. She always chose her words carefully and waited for the right moment. 'Red', she said, 'it might allow you to go back to some lovely places.' A murmur from AW and a puff on the pipe. 'And you do quite like Richard. I think we can trust him.' No murmur of assent this time but the slightest of nods. I knew Betty was keen for the series to go ahead, thinking that it might give Wainwright a new lease of life and an additional interest at a time when his eyesight was becoming problematic.

Earlier, Betty had given me one piece of advice. Now she looked at me and nodded. It was time to act on that information. 'I don't suppose it will make a difference but there is one other thing I forgot to mention. There would be a little money for you and Betty and it could go to Animal Rescue.' In an instant I had AW's complete attention and for good reason. Animal Rescue Cumbria was in need of immediate support after a difficult year. There had been unscheduled staff changes and building work had strained its finances. My offer was a tempting one. It was important never to rush AW, so my aim on this visit was to get any answer other than an outright 'no'. I drove home pleased with the day's work and thankful for Betty's support.

On my next visit a number of maps were spread out and I was taking notes. I had been summoned to the house after a phone call from Betty informed me that AW was happy to talk about possible locations. Over a period of weeks AW set out his plan.

He had clearly enjoyed the process of planning the five programmes we were going to make. He was good at choosing locations, suggesting routes and places to visit, but less good at how a documentary film is constructed. AW thought in terms of individual shots rather than a number of scenes and, old-fashioned as it might appear, a beginning, a middle and an end. Over time I would try to quietly slip in some of these additions. My method was a suggestion here and there, always trying to do so in a way that AW would find acceptable. It turned into a game of cat and mouse: sometimes Wainwright would adopt my suggestions, but not too often and if he felt I was in danger of getting too much of my own way, then he would call a halt. This was not simply the result of a power play or someone who wanted to be entirely in control. What drove Wainwright was not immediately obvious, but even then I sensed it was involuntary and came from somewhere deep within him.

In fact, AW never said 'yes' to the series but having reached agreement about where we might visit and what dates might be suitable (including avoiding his annual fortnight in Scotland), contracts were signed, hotels reserved, the film crew booked and the whole painstaking process of making television programmes set in motion.

There had however been one big obstacle still to overcome in the weeks leading up to the start of filming; one that I spent days agonising over. I had been told that Eric Robson should present the new series. Eric had, quite deservedly, a high profile and had recently moved back to Cumbria after a spell in Manchester presenting a succession of programmes that had attracted a lot of attention. Now he was also becoming established as the face of our region. He's an exceptionally accomplished presenter and a skilful interviewer. He started out in the Carlisle studios of Border Television as an assistant floor manager (allegedly after a highly successful previous career as a removals man) and this training has served him well. He has a sixth sense about where the camera might be that is invaluable when filming. As a young, inexperienced producer, I relied on Eric and learnt enormously from him. He was, and still is, a consummate professional.

Given AW's love of routine and order, I knew it would be hard to explain why we now had a new presenter. At the end of my visit, I broached the topic with Wainwright. I stressed that Eric, in spite of being born north of the border, was Cumbrian through and through. The conversation was not going as well as I would have liked. AW remained suspicious of this apparent interloper. What I could not tell him was that Eric was an archetypal entrepreneur. Stand still for a few moments and Eric will try and sell you something; outline his latest plans or explain how you can double your income or more with no effort on your part. At this time Eric had just taken over the tenancy of a National Trust farm not far from Nether Wasdale and had great plans for it, the first of which was the production of sausages from rare breed Tamworth pigs. For some months it was necessary to buy a pound or two of these sausages before Eric's attention could be engaged. As a vegetarian, it was then necessary for me to find them a good home. Eric's farming exploits were not entirely trouble-free either: some time later they were to lead to an armed response team descending on the farm when a pig escaped and an alarmed walker reported gunshots coming from the surrounding land.

Yet Eric's farming credentials, slim as they were at that time, did help when AW said he did not care for television presenters who were too full of their own importance. Seizing the moment, I quickly replied, 'But that's why Eric's such a good choice, he's a Cumbrian farmer who just does a bit of television...'.

The idea for the series was a simple one: Wainwright would show us five of his favourite places. Lakeland, Teesdale and the Howgill Fells would come later, but we would start in spring, in the land of the Yorkshire Three Peaks, north of Settle. We began with an ascent of that fine freestanding summit, Pen-y-ghent. (An apology is due here: AW did not like the hyphens used by the Ordnance Survey. His main reason undoubtedly sprang from his own experience of calligraphy when he found them an irritation. Sorry AW, but I'm sticking with the OS on this one, although you will be pleased to know that the suffix 'hill' no longer appears on their maps.)

AW thought spring would be a good time to be on the mountain with the purple saxifrage decorating the higher reaches and, visiting in midweek, it would be less crowded than at weekends or during the summer months. We had chosen Pen-y-ghent at Wainwright's request and the reasons for this told me a lot about his character. He had thought we would be able to work without being noticed by other hillgoers. Although I had assured him this should not be a major problem, he insisted we start here. He was worried about being recognised in the Lakes and thought he would be lesser known in the Yorkshire Dales. This turned out to be the least of my problems.

Pen-y-ghent... and the TV licence fee

In England, it is necessary when filming to obtain permission from the landowner. Many will be very helpful but you are never sure what response you will get when you make that initial telephone call. Indeed, strange as it may seem, it is sometimes difficult to establish who the landowner might be. Pen-y-ghent had its own difficulties with a number of people owning different parts of the hill and surrounding area. Working my way through this list, I ended up one evening in a remote farmhouse on the fellside with the farmer. His family had worked these hills for generations and he was a Yorkshireman to the bone. We started our conversation like two boxers sparring, trying to get the measure of each other. I talked about an uncle who had worked the land, but how poor wages, a damp tied house and bleak prospects had forced him down the pit. The pay was infinitely better but life expectancy much shorter and he had died a few years earlier, still short of his fiftieth birthday. This led to a discussion of sheep farming in the dales and its own problems.

Eventually it became clear that the farmer would have no objection to our filming, but the contentious question of a suitable payment still remained. I also wanted to drive my Land Rover over his land, which would almost certainly put the price up. I was still thinking about what we might be able to offer, when the farmer put down his mug of tea and stared me in the face. 'And would you believe it,' he said, 'those buggers at the BBC have just put up my telly licence again'. He was right. Just a month earlier there had been a huge hike in the cost of a colour television from £34 to £58 reflecting the inflation rate. Suddenly I had a thought. 'How would you feel if I paid you the difference?', I asked. Thinking this was a finger up to authority, my host readily agreed and the deal was done. It was a bargain.

When we arrived to film, I mentioned this to AW. 'Quite right too', he said, and thinking back to his accountancy days, 'I think there's always room for economy'.

It was a sunny day with a cold wind blowing from the east. I had gained permission to take my Land Rover a good way along the track to Hull Pot which considerably shortened the route. Even so, I was concerned about how AW would manage the ascent. His poor eyesight had been evident from the first time I met him and he talked to me at length about his inability to see detail – either on a map or the landscape in front of him. He was unable to resolve the contour lines, symbols and many names on OS maps and, as any walker well knows, these are the bedrock of navigation. However, two quite different aspects of Wainwright's relationship with the landscape began to emerge that day. Firstly, he had committed vast tracts of it to memory. The detail with which he had done so impressed me. I am not talking about the big sweep of valleys and hills, but innumerable intimate details which he could retrieve when required. Secondly, in the lead-up to our filming, AW had realised these maps were as important to me as to him, so he entrusted me to guide him through them. He would want to know whether an awkward step still existed, or if the way through a farmyard was still confusing. Did today's maps still contain an error he had spotted years ago, or was a recently renovated footbridge still in the same location? What I found most revealing was this exceptional micro-level knowledge of a landscape he might not have visited in many years. There was always a precision about these questions: was a telephone box still there or what was the current state of a cairn? Usually he would be following up information sent in by followers of his work, sometimes months or even years previously. 'I'm told that it is no longer possible to get to the fell this way, but I'm not sure that's correct', would be a typical comment.

It was not just AW's poor eyesight that was foremost in my mind as we made our way up the eroded track on the western flank of Pen-y-ghent. Years of continuous smoking accompanied by a diet that, in spite of Betty's best efforts, was a nutritionist's nightmare had resulted in him putting on weight. As AW, Betty, camera crew, Eric Robson and myself made our way up the track, I was looking at a man who was clearly top heavy and moved quite slowly. Yet for someone who was 78, he was still able to make steady progress and we reached the summit by about noon.

I was impressed by this and, most importantly, Wainwright was in good spirits and pleased with his achievement. Failing eyesight or not, he was able to recite the summit panorama to the team without omitting any details. Sadly it was not the clearest of days, so we missed out on seeing the Lake District hills, although they were as clear as ever in AW's mind's eye.

The start of our filming on Pen-y-ghent. Whilst AW was reclining against the summit cairn pleased to have made the ascent, Eric was less relaxed than he might appear. He had just been told by our star, 'Just remember... you don't know who I am yet...'

We had agreed that our filming would begin on the summit and finish in Horton in Ribblesdale (no hyphens here to trouble AW), laid out some 450 or so metres beneath us. Of course Wainwright, as he told us, didn't recognise metres, so on this occasion, I'll add that it's getting on for 1,500 feet lower down. We did not get off to quite the start I had envisaged. AW lay, rather than sat, on the summit cairn and Eric had little option but to join him. While I was fretting, our camera person, John

Warwick, was impressed by this surreal beginning. However, the filming was about to get infinitely more difficult. AW had a rigid plan for the film. He revealed this to me a week or so previously and it set alarm bells ringing.

Wainwright's grand idea was this: he would be on the summit of Pen-y-ghent and Eric would arrive there. The two would start chatting and then descend together. There was nothing wrong with this except for one extremely large problem. Eric would pretend not to have recognised or know that he was in the company of AW. The two would walk down together chatting away and finally reach the car park in Horton. In the course of saying their goodbyes Eric would thank his anonymous walking companion for a good day out. This would be the cue for me, in the style of Alfred Hitchcock, to enter my own film. I would walk into the scene and say, 'Hello AW. How are you? It's good to see you again.' Eric would then look at me and AW and with feigned incredulity speak lines that AW had scripted for him.

There was no way out. We had to follow AW's instructions, although I knew that this would never be shown to the nation on BBC2. I also guessed it was beyond even Eric's undoubted thespian tendencies to deliver what AW had planned. I wondered how the camera could possibly film an open-jawed Eric who, after a few seconds of stunned silence, is finally able to shock himself into coherence to utter the film's final, supposedly immortal words. 'AW? It can't be, can it? Is it you? I had no idea, AW – the great fell walker. It's you!' I also thought Eric might also need to produce a fake swoon at this point.

My 'solution' was to try to make two films in tandem: the one Wainwright had so carefully scripted and the one that would be broadcast on BBC2. John Warwick was chuckling and intrigued about how the day would develop. Eric, as always, thought there would be no problem. In fact there was one very big problem. Walking down from the summit Eric tried to talk to AW about his life and his work. No sooner had Eric managed a question than there was an immediate response from our star: 'Eric, you can't ask me that yet... you don't know who I am'. The look on Eric's face was priceless. We made our way down, moving from the gritstone of the summit to the limestone lower down, with AW sticking rigidly to *his* film every step of the way. And, yes, that final scene in the Horton car park has long since been consigned to the dustbin.

But if I could not give AW the finale he wanted, I think the start of the film did do justice to him. It was a dramatic entrance on the summit plateau, especially when AW discarded his cap and lit his pipe. I found that a hugely emotional moment; the man who we had called, 'folk hero to tens of thousands of fellwalkers' was now sharing his love of high places with the camera. A man who, for 50 years, had been a solitary, elusive figure in the fells, someone whose self-portraits in each of his seven-volume *Guide* only ever showed a back view, was finally coming out of the shadows. What he said was equally important and set the tone for what would follow. 'I suppose really I could be described as a backroom boy. I don't like being pushed onto a stage. I've never got rid of my Lancashire accent. I wouldn't like to have to stand up in front of a lot of people and talk... That's not my line *at all*... No, I'm better at writing than talking...'.

Before this first programme of our new series was broadcast there would be months of heartache. As we gently made our way back to Horton, my plan of trying to make two parallel films simultaneously was proving to be disastrous. There were some wonderful moments, not least by the summit cairn when, pulling a BBC flask out of my borrowed rucksack, Eric spoke to his supposedly unknown companion about the joys of solitary walking. I had just about managed to convince AW that answering such a question would not give the game away. Likewise there was an informal mood in Wainwright's conversation and, aided by a soft light, a wonderful quality to John Warwick's photography. And it did not take long before AW's idiosyncratic character began to shine through. It only needed Eric to ask about the height of Pen-y-ghent and AW was in full flow, 'The top is 2273. Feet. Not metres. I don't recognise metres... I don't accept metres...so everything's feet with me... Great Gable has been demoted to something under a thousand now. I think it's disgraceful. It's an affront to Great Gable not to be nearly 3000 feet...' The most memorable moment came by the side of Hunt Pot where the entrance has a sheer drop of 200 feet onto the bedrock below. Eric asked if he might take a closer look at the entrance. 'You'll have to be careful', came the reply, 'You'll never get out if you get in there. We won't bother with you...', and as a final thought on the subject, 'I've never been anywhere where it's been too difficult or too dangerous, which is one reason why I've lived so long.'

However, these witty asides were no more than brief interludes, for much of the time AW either said little or reminded Eric that he did not yet know his identity. Meanwhile the film crew were trying to suppress their laughter. I saw no alternative but to battle bravely on. We filmed innumerable evocative wide shots of the pair walking, wondering how we would ever manage to piece a film together. Finally late in the afternoon and with *Coronation Street* beckoning, we filmed the final scene in Horton car park and the big denouement. Eric Robson's final words to me as the gear was packed away are still engraved on my brain: 'You will never... ever... get a film out of this'.

AW enjoyed the day we had together exploring Pen-y-ghent and was keen to talk about its many distinctive features, especially the two most prominent pot holes, Hunt Pot and Hull Pot. At that time, I didn't know that he had first visited the latter at the start of his long Pennine walk in 1938.

THE RELUCTANT STAR

An improbable fashion icon

There were never any continuity problems when filming with AW. We did not have a star who came with an extensive wardrobe or a person who wore a blue jumper one day and a red one the next. Betty had bought him some new clothes at the start of our filming and these were worn, with only minor changes, from then on, with his jumper, trousers and jacket acquiring more burn marks as the years progressed. His boots were always done up in the same old-fashioned way with the laces taken twice around the ankles, socks were partially exposed and trousers tucked into them. His rucksack and flat cap were ubiquitous accompaniments. I worried about him getting overheated on hot days and hypothermic when the weather turned nasty, but AW was oblivious to all this. He was more focused about his trusty supply of Three Nuns tobacco. When the pipe wasn't lit or being sucked on, then it was time for a cigarette. He and Eric were a well suited pair.

Only the worst weather would make us seek shelter – times when it was futile to continue in the face of driving rain and high winds or when our concern for AW meant we had to call a halt and get him out of a deluge. Sometimes that meant retreating to the shelter of a car. If Eric invited AW into his car, the results were predictable. After 20 minutes or so, the interior was entirely fog-bound with two figures barely discernible through a haze of cigarette and pipe smoke, each encouraging the other. At the top of Honister Pass I went over to them and, trying to see inside, I wondered what was least damaging to Wainwright – being outside in the wind and wet or inside in what looked like a schoolboy dare to see who could smoke the most. When Betty made her view clear to AW, he had the look of a teenager caught behind the bike sheds. There's a postscript to this note on fashion. Never one to be outdone, Eric had a pair of tweed plus-fours that could stand up by themselves and a waxed jacket with bits of baler twine in the pockets along with other sundry odds and ends. Today both would be an obvious health and safety hazard. I heard recently that Eric's long-suffering partner, Annette, had secretly disposed of the legwear much to Eric's consternation. As AW might say, 'Another bit of Lakeland history gone forever'.

Little wonder that Eric and AW got on so well.

4. Wainwright
as seen on TV

What followed during the remainder of that 1985 summer was to set a pattern for all our subsequent filming: a discussion about the next film and the possible locations; then my recces to see if this would work on television and if we could obtain landowners' permission to film. There followed more meetings with AW to explain how the research was going. The culmination of this was the week's filming itself. We had often not reached a final agreement before we set off with the film crew and Eric. My strategy was always to leave some aspects unresolved and, at all costs, to avoid a firm 'no' from Wainwright. In marked contrast Derry Brabbs, the photographer, who illustrated most of the books originally published by Michael Joseph, was issued with a set of instructions. With these in hand he bravely went out to try and fulfil AW's orders. That relationship was replicated with many others AW worked with, not least the *Westmorland Gazette*, who always had to follow his commands.

I see a film as a cooperative endeavour but Wainwright found this difficult, especially at first. Betty was pivotal in formulating a way for us to work together. If AW had made a firm decision, even she could find him immovable, but she had a wonderful insight into his character and her power of persuasion was significant. If I wanted agreement on anything that might be unusual or contentious, I always asked Betty first. Given Wainwright's fixed views, I was surprised we had relatively few disagreements, although some of these could be serious. Once when we were arguing, AW pointedly asked *exactly* what I did. I was saved from an incoherent reply by Betty who jumped into the conversation. 'That's not fair, Red. You know how much Richard does to make these films a success. You should be grateful to him'.

It was only then that I understood how different my relationship was with Wainwright from that of others. He found discussion difficult and the art of compromise even more taxing. I remember Betty telling us, 'you both have to compromise. Red, you need to *listen* to what Richard is saying – he has your best interests at heart. Richard, I think Red has a point here – consider it carefully. Now would you like more tea and coffee?' AW and I would look at each other, both suitably chastened. The only comment from AW: 'Betty has spoken...'

In May 1985 we started with a week's filming around Haweswater. We began on Monday morning at the northern end of the dam but opposite the public road and in the shadow of Bampton Common. We were making slow but steady progress. I was worried about a weather forecast that predicted a low front coming in from the west and bringing the inevitable rain in its wake. Those predictions were 100% accurate and early on Tuesday afternoon progress was halted. We were faced with heavy rain that looked set in for the rest of the day. It was impossible to continue filming in these conditions and, seeking shelter as quickly as possible, we ended up in the lounge of the Haweswater Hotel. In retrospect, it turned out to be a wonderful blessing. It was early in the season and we had the room to ourselves. I was still not entirely sure what I was doing but aware that I should be doing something, knowing that, left to their own devices, there was a good chance Eric and the film crew would get up to mischief. I did not want any impromptu poker games taking place in front of Betty and AW and I also needed to have some results to show for our day's work. I suggested that it might be useful if Eric were to talk to AW, explaining that anything he said here could be used with images we would shoot when the weather improved. Wainwright was expecting to talk about this particular part of Lakeland, but I whispered to Eric, 'Ask him about his early life and himself'. In directing Eric in this way, I knew what only one other person knew... and it was not good news.

Producing a documentary shot on 16mm film is a world removed from the way almost all television is made today. In 1985 the exposed film had to be sent away to a lab, where it was developed and a cutting copy made from the negative. Some days later this film arrived back at the BBC. This then had to be synchronised with the sound which itself had been transferred from the original audio tape. It could be a week or more before you had a chance to look at the material you had shot.

Today, images and audio are recorded electronically onto small solid state cards. These are then transferred to a computer, where viewing the material and editing can begin immediately. Material can be moved from one part of a film to another at the click of a mouse and sophisticated effects can be added by simply selecting a preset. The accountants who now dominate television love this: it appears to be more efficient, it is scheduled to take fewer weeks and, most importantly, it costs less and budgets can therefore be reduced. When filming Wainwright it was very different. A roll of film was loaded into a magazine and lasted ten minutes and 40 seconds. Sound was recorded on audio tape that, inconveniently, lasted 15 minutes. The film was also a fixed cost – once exposed that was it, it couldn't be reused.

This gave rise to a certain tension. Imagine, for example, recording an interview. The first few minutes are not especially interesting and, as they are being recorded, you know they have little likelihood of being used in the final film.

However, after about nine minutes the interviewee is warmed up and begins to reveal exciting and important information. Two minutes later they could be in full flow but at this moment the film will run out. A harassed director has two choices: stop the conversation and hope that it can be repeated when a new magazine loaded with fresh film is inserted in the camera or continue to record, but only on audio knowing that there are just four minutes before that tape also comes to an end. Sometimes the camera assistant would quickly put another magazine in the camera so filming could continue immediately, but we would soon be waiting for the sound tape to be changed – which was a more lengthy process. To make all this even more convoluted, any material recorded solely on audio tape would need to be used with images shot elsewhere. If someone was talking about a mountain this could be quite easy, at other times it could more problematic. Occasionally it could be a nightmare. Sitting in an editing room you would discover that the beginning of a story, recorded on one roll of film, didn't match the conclusion, recorded on another. The permutations were almost endless, but editing this series with AW was to take it to an entirely new level.

The interview with AW in our original documentary with David Bean had given me a false sense of security. Our programme had been designed around him *not* appearing, so it was a relatively simple matter to introduce him near the end of it, helped, of course, by the exclusive nature of this first television appearance. Additionally, with AW fully rehearsed and word perfect, we had fitted in with his predetermined plan. But this new series was different. Here Wainwright was the central figure – a man, in the twilight of his life, taking the viewer to the places that had shaped his love affair with our great outdoors.

After our first filming on Pen-y-ghent, our film editor and associate producer, Ian Sutherland, had looked at what we had shot with the aim of making a rough selection of the best material. At least that was the theory. Ian was a recent arrival to Newcastle but had gained experience in the drama department at BBC Birmingham. He knew how to craft a compelling story and was good company in the confined space of an editing room. We would be spending most of the next six months working together, so getting on well was a great bonus.

In theory there is no great mystique to editing a film. You simply select the best material – compelling conversation and iconic images – and stitch the two together. It is no more difficult than baking a cake. Various other components can also be added to taste: the use of narrator, music, graphics etc. In practice it is considerably more complicated and, in the case of Wainwright, infinitely more challenging. Yet all films start out from the same place, by reviewing everything that has been shot, making notes on it and literally cutting out the best bits and hanging them in a 'trim bin' – in effect a dustbin with a metal scaffold above it with two arms containing numerous small metal hooks. Each individual piece of film is hung up scene by scene with an assistant making a record of what is where. There is one trick that often surprises those new to the editing process – the clips are selected on the basis of the sound and what is being said. Only later are the final images that will illustrate this placed in to give the film its final and, hopefully, polished appearance.

After our Pen-y-ghent shoot Ian Sutherland laboured valiantly away. We were aiming to produce a first assembly which would later progress to a rough cut and finally, after many bacon rolls and coffee, mysteriously morph into a finished film. Looking at the maths, if a final film is a nominal 30 minutes, the rough cut might be 40 to 45 minutes and the first assembly nearer 60 minutes or even longer. After a week or so toiling on this new project, Ian Sutherland summoned me back to his edit room to announce that, together, we had achieved a world record for a first assembly of a documentary film. 'Guess how long it is', said Ian. A grin that was nearer to hysteria than a smile hinted this might not be the answer I was expecting, but it was important to keep up appearances and show no sign of weakness. 'I don't know', and wishing to not appear unduly concerned, added 'What? About 40 minutes?' Ian pointed to a meagre amount of film laced up on the editing machine. 'THAT', he emphasised, 'THAT is exactly 8½ minutes'. Me: 'It could be worse'. (Although quite how, I wasn't sure.) Ian, echoing John Laurie's portrayal of Private Frazer in *Dad's Army*, looked at the small reel on his editing machine and said simply: 'We're doomed. We're all doomed'. It was Friday afternoon, so I suggested we think about it over the weekend, having no clear idea about how that might help and how we had any hope of turning 8½ minutes into a fully fledged documentary. Perhaps, if we repeated it three times and added a bit, the problem would be solved.

St Sunday Crag is a Lakeland favourite of mine. Situated in the eastern lakes, it was easily accessible from our Pennine home and, with two young children, it made for an expedition full of interest and achievement.

That Saturday we made our way to the summit of St Sunday Crag, then spent time wandering around to get the best views of Fairfield, Helvellyn and our old favourite, High Street. It was a bright, airy day with relatively few people around. As we descended to Grisedale Tarn I left the family behind and began to think about what I was calling *The Wainwright Problem* or, more specifically, what I could find to make some sort of half decent film. I considered the positives, thinking how lucky I was to work with Wainwright. I wondered how many envious filmmakers would want to swap places with me. But these thoughts were quickly outweighed by the negatives. I had achieved all this only to be faced with the prospect of having films that were – at least on the current evidence – unfit to be broadcast. Having reached a mental stalemate my mind began to wander.

I've never been a particular fan of football, but I do love those phrases you hear whenever the game is broadcast – a set of stock clichés that never cease to amaze me. *It's a game of two halves* is a perennial favourite, along with *It isn't over until it's over*. For some reason that is still unfathomable all these years later, that latter phrase lodged itself in my mind and I began to apply it to my problem. Three miles of walking remained down Grisedale and with each step a plan began to emerge. I thought, firstly, about how the films should look when they were broadcast. We needed Wainwright and Eric talking about where they were and what they had seen, but also AW in more reflective mood explaining his motivation and his philosophy. I wanted to hear the story of how he came to Kendal from crowded Lancashire and noisy Blackburn; I needed him to talk about how the books were produced, page by loving page, and the 13-year plan that had underpinned their creation. Above all, I wanted the sense of having been at his side on this remarkable journey – a journey that must rank as one of the most ambitious ever undertaken by a landscape writer.

Such conversation would, I guessed, be best conducted in calm surroundings and with an air of privacy. Then there was Wainwright's prose: in his many guides it is often more akin to poetry. Why not have some of it read in the films? Why not accompany these readings with his meticulous drawings and the handwritten text that give the books their unique hallmark? Finally we needed a sense of place – the landscape within which AW had tramped to and fro and which was both the raw material and inspiration for his life's work. Put all this together and we might, just might, end up with the kind of film I had originally envisaged.

Betty was asking me about the progress of the film and it was clear that she shared my concern about how we were getting on. Just before we started filming in the Haweswater Hotel she had spoken to AW and suggested his answers could be more fulsome than previously. Of course, filming in a hotel lounge is a poor substitute for the wonderful Lakeland panorama as a backdrop but John Warwick thought he could make it work and Wainwright had taken a liking to John, who was not an outdoors person but a quirky figure – someone who, more often than not, wore immaculate white plimsolls. (Plimsolls that were still clean after our day on Pen-y-ghent. At my insistence, he made an exception and swapped them for walking boots for the ascent of Haystacks.)

I also needed to enthuse Eric Robson. Eric is an exceptionally talented interviewer and presenter, but was clearly becoming frustrated when well thought through questions received little more than a 'yes' or 'no' in answer, or, worst of all, just silence and the puffing of a pipe. With no expectations about getting anything we might be able to use, Eric followed my instructions and asked AW to think back over 60 years to his early life. It wasn't unusual for there to be a long pause between Eric's question and any possible response. During this time – which could be as long as half a minute, everyone was in suspense as to what, if anything, might happen, or what AW would say.

And then AW started to speak: about his parents; the house in which he grew up; his school years; and what he thought life would be like after he left school.

One of my favourite photographs of AW, but this may be coloured by the circumstances under which I took it. In the deserted lounge of the Haweswater Hotel, AW had just spent 20 minutes talking movingly about his early life in Blackburn. When he finished I knew, for the first time, we could make our films work.

Twenty minutes later he was still talking, only interrupted by our need to change film magazines and sound tapes. Set against the background of our previous filming in which he'd said very little, this was exactly what we needed. Eric caught my eye and I could see he was also relieved. After all, there isn't much demand for interviewers who can't solicit answers from their subjects.

Wainwright paused and Eric was about to ask a follow-up question. It would doubtless have been relevant and succinct, but AW had decided he had told us enough for one day. Looking away from Eric and across to me he said, 'That'll do for today, Richard. You've got what you need. I think we'll go home now'. This was the nearest I ever came to hugging him.

AW had spoken about his early life in a matter-of-fact way that all of us found deeply compelling. The conversation moved on from those early years to the Lakeland he knew during the time he'd been writing his *Guide*. He was visibly relaxed in the privacy of the hotel lounge and started to explain what he had found so fascinating about this landscape. 'I was always concerned more with the mountains than the valleys. I never spent much time in the valleys, I was always on the tops and of course the tops don't change. They are exactly as I remember them 50 years ago when I first started coming here. So they're not really out of date. The routes of ascent are still the same.'

So behind what were seemingly leisurely conversations between Eric and Wainwright there lay a trick. Some of the sound was recorded on location but much was captured later, often indoors and at times when AW was relaxed. Those memorable scenes where the pair are placed within a landscape and moving away from the camera are a hallmark of the films, but they were born out of necessity. Walking away from the lens means that you cannot see what they might be saying and, providing the body language is right and the words appropriate, conversations recorded at a entirely different time and place can be inserted.

Wainwright also had an uncanny ability to wrongfoot us. On a sunny afternoon later in the week he was sitting on Mardale Common with that magnificent view west to Riggindale Ridge, the bowl of Blea Water and the summit of High Street. It is, especially in winter, one of my favourite spots in the whole of Lakeland and I'd said this to AW. Yet when the camera was running Wainwright made the bold claim that here was the finest valley head, placing it above other obvious contenders like Langdale and Wasdale, although admitting it might not be as grand. I found this odd given that Haweswater reservoir is a manmade construction and one that AW felt had ruined what he remembered as a beautiful, isolated valley. 'Destroyed' was the word he used. Perhaps it was the fate of this valley and the eviction of the Mardale residents or a landscape that represented a vanished Lakeland, but for whatever reason this return visit deeply affected Wainwright.

Yet this week's filming had a more fundamental impact for me. It marked a clear turning point in the way AW and I worked together. Later Wainwright was to tell friends that he was beginning to enjoy the filming process, although one chance comment or minor complaint to him was likely to reverse the process. He was enjoying sharing his knowledge of this landscape with a new audience and explaining the motivation behind his most important work: 'I thought, there'll come a time when I'll not be able to do these walks so I'll make a record of them and that's the way it started really, in 1952. I started to detail all the climbs that I'd done, all the details of the fells, getting everything ready for when I was an old man and confined to a chair. Now I'm an old man, my eyes are going, I can't read the books that I did then, so it wasn't exactly a waste of effort because I thoroughly enjoyed doing them, but the fruits of what I did are not obtained by looking at the books again and going through them because I can't see them. The fruits of the work have been in the success of the books.'

Which, of course, begs the question of whether his books had been responsible for the influx of visitors that, in the view of some people, was spoiling the Lake District. For once, AW did not struggle to find an answer. He told us, 'I've been accused of having encouraged too many people but I don't think that's true. I think people would come anyway. The world of commerce today and business is getting such a problem that this is an escape and I think more people are finding that. So I don't attach any blame to myself for that. I think probably I've given a lot of pleasure to people who may never have ventured up because of course there were no detailed guidebooks to the fells until I did them. No, I have nothing to reproach myself about that.'

I felt our choice of films for the first series was a curious one. In addition to our ascent of Pen-y-ghent and the filming around Haweswater, we had decided to make one based around a section of the Pennine Way and another in the Howgill Fells, leaving a final film to conclude the series.

AW did not relate to the Pennine Way in the instinctive way he empathised with the Lake District. Even allowing for the bad weather that accompanied many of his journeys along sections of it, he found much of it featureless and boring. The finest section, at least at far as AW was concerned, is almost 25 miles long and runs from Upper Teesdale to Great Dun Fell on the Pennine watershed. On that journey upstream there are many impressive features, both natural and manmade. They include Low and High Force. The latter he said, 'is the Tees' finest moment' and the biggest waterfall in the country. What he did reveal on that journey up to Cauldron Snout was the exact way in which he worked. 'It was me, a camera and the 2½-inch map that I was working on at that time. The notes I made on the map. I didn't carry a notebook. In fact I was checking the route on the map all the time and indicating where there were stiles and gates and a choice of alternatives and so on. All that was done by making notes on the map as I went along.'

Later AW let me borrow these maps so I could film them. I was surprised by the sheer amount of detailed notes AW had added to each map. This went far beyond brief annotation. There were dozens of comments, all carefully added in red ink. They included descriptions: 'short grass, but no path', was a typical example. Stiles, gates, walls and a choice of alternative route were all neatly inscribed. Sometimes he recorded revisiting a specific location to ensure his description would be accurate. Many of these places were very remote so the effort required to do this was substantial. In the short distance around Great Dun Fell and Little Dun Fell there are no fewer than 12 substantial annotations. The bottom of the map was also covered with longer notes. Although Wainwright had four helpers who did much of the preliminary research for the Pennine Way book, it is nonetheless breathtaking to see the level of detail applied to every one of the route's 270 miles.

Wainwright spoke to me about how the main body of the book worked. The strip map was the backbone, after which came the text and then any illustrations necessary to balance the page. In talking of 'balancing', it was clear he regarded his books as works of art, above and beyond accurate cartography or carefully crafted prose. During the time I had these original maps it became evident AW's work went far beyond what is required of a diligent author keen to check his facts. I was left thinking this was almost an obsession – one that was all-consuming and dominated his life.

A month later we were on the Howgill Fells. In 1985 they were rarely visited and we talked again about Wainwright's relationship with the Ordnance Survey maps that had been the inspiration for his work. While they served as an all-important starting point, giving AW a sense of what the landscape would look like before he began to explore it in detail, he never accepted them at face value. 'Checking on the Ordnance maps' was the description he used and considerable satisfaction was gained on the rare occasions when his observations proved the OS had made a mistake. That happened on the Howgills, 'They had one particular height as 1700 (feet) and I realised from neighbouring summits that it was higher than where I was at 1900. I finally wrote to them and said, "You've made a mistake with this particular height". They sent a man up to check and I was right. It should have been 1970 feet or something like that. And then in a few cases I don't agree with the contours because they're not meticulously surveyed'. Even so, Wainwright was still in awe of the mapmakers' achievement.

One morning we were in AW's sitting room and I remembered that Andrew Nichol, the *Westmorland Gazette*'s printing manager, always visited him there. I asked if he had ever returned the favour and gone to see Andrew in his office. 'No... I never have', was the reply. 'But you've seen your books being printed I presume?' 'No. I've been asked often enough but I've never been there'. I found it strange that someone who had invested so much in his *Guide*, even allowing his first marriage, in his own words, to 'wither', and was so particular as to how they should look, had not taken the trouble to see them come off the press. In 30 years he had not once popped into the *Gazette* printing works. 'He's an absolute stranger to our staff', was Andrew's comment. Curiously, it did not need much persuasion on my part to suggest we might make that first visit in the company of Eric and the cameras. During the course of our conversation with Andrew, Wainwright did admit there is a spelling mistake in one of his books and was pleased that no one appeared to have spotted it. He was more ambivalent when Andrew told of a group of farmers who had been given a conducted tour of the works some time previously. One said that AW's guide contained an instruction to turn left at a green gate but the farmer proudly announced, 'I've fixed the buggers... I've painted all bloody gates black'.

Star Treatment on Cross Fell

One scene that sadly never appeared in our Pennine Way film was on Cross Fell. This is a place that, for much of the year, is bleak, windswept moorland but, on good days, is transformed into an elemental landscape full of power and grandeur, where humans can appear as insignificant dots on a much bigger canvas. We managed to get permission to drive up the private road to Great Dun Fell and our plan was to cross Little Dun Fell and walk to the highest point — Cross Fell. The weather was not good and the wind did little to help the filming. It was a lot of effort for little reward and I knew we would not get enough material for a coherent scene. While we were making our decision to cut our losses and head back, AW and Eric sheltered by a cairn to have a hot drink. Shortly after, a walker appeared and seeing the film cameras asked, 'Are you Wainwright?'. Immediately AW looked up from his cup of tea and answered, 'One of us might be'. And that was the end of the conversation.

AW immediately after his encounter with the hapless fellwalker.

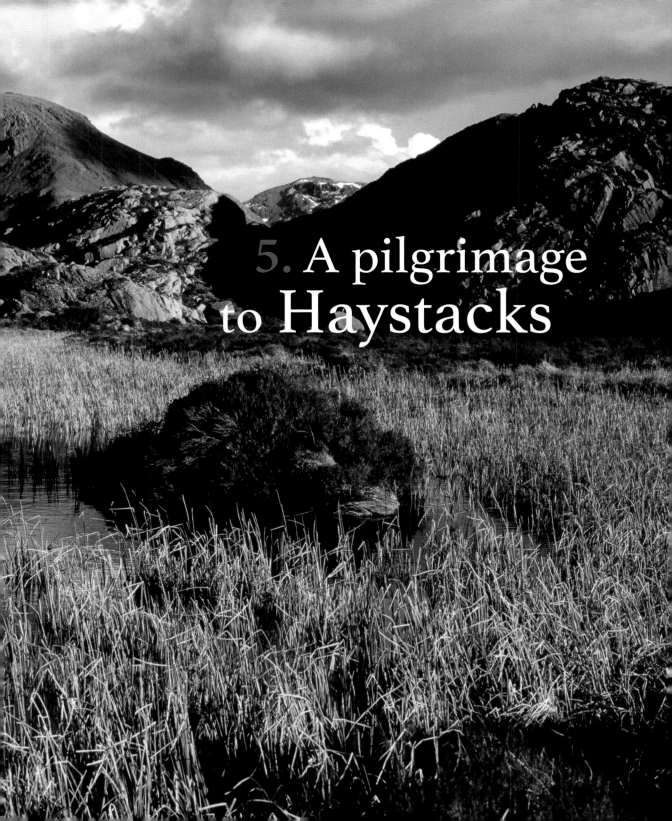

5. A pilgrimage to Haystacks

A pilgrimage to Haystacks. Innominate Tarn on an early spring evening with still a bite in the air. I almost inevitably spent the night here, pitching my lightweight tent near the summit of Haystacks. More than once, AW asked why I did that. The first part of my answer was always the same, 'Because it's too good a place to leave'. That got a nod of approval.

At the end of a long and very wet day, I was exhausted. We had done it. I couldn't quite believe it. Wainwright had made an emotional and, as is now well known, final journey to the place he loved above all others. It has become the most important of all the sequences we filmed with him. Yet it was not part of our original plan. Or, more accurately, it was not part of AW's plan for our first series. I had always hoped we could visit Haystacks but there were numerous difficulties to overcome. Not least of these was AW's reluctance to be filmed in Lakeland and a fear that numerous walkers would want to stop and talk to their hero. Our previous filming around Haweswater had been agreed because of the relative remoteness of that valley. In 1985 the car park was still small and, outside of weekends, high summer and bank holidays, it was possible to walk in this area without attracting much attention. Wainwright was amenable to this filming but he had, on more than one occasion, politely yet firmly declined my suggestions for visiting other places in Lakeland.

As our filming progressed I noticed a number of changes gradually taking place. Our star was – on a good day, at least – more at ease with the filming process; he grew fond of the camera team and began to feel more at ease with them – after all, it was clear they had specific and necessary skills, while it was unclear what I as producer and director contributed (if anything). There was another key factor. Betty enjoyed having new people to talk to and was fascinated by our very different backgrounds. Best of all, she said, was AW being able to visit places they both thought he would not see again.

Before long the cold winds of spring gave way to the longer, warmer days of summer, but my interest was less with the weather than in waiting for the right moment to talk to AW.

Oh dear... Stirred, shaken, noisy and with no creature comforts, AW and Eric make their way up the old quarry track above Honister. Shortly afterwards all mechanical progress was halted as the vehicle and one of its tracks parted company.

I knew I would only get one chance to raise this particular subject and that any rejection would be final. Eventually, and trying hard to conceal my nervousness, I thought the moment might have arrived. My visits to Kendal Green followed a set pattern: coffee and cakes from Betty; an agreement of what we would be doing next (always the trickiest bit); AW asking where I had been recently and what my plans were; any news that he and Betty had for me; and then a pause before we went for that Little Chef lunch. This particular visit was going well. I explained how the films were beginning to take shape and how I thought he and Betty would enjoy them. Back in the cutting room Ian Sutherland was labouring away and, thanks to his Herculean efforts, I could finally see something resembling a finished programme.

We were about to finish our meeting and AW was asking what time it was, making it clear that the all-important lunch must be the next item on the agenda. The accountant in him was pleased when I pointed out that not only would there be the fee he donated to Animal Rescue Cumbria, but, if he added all my visits up, the Little Chef meals I treated him to would exceed what he paid for his licence fee.

'It can always get worse', is a motto I have always found useful - and inevitably true. The predicted rain had started in earnest, the wind was strengthening and the climb up to Innominate Tarn still lay ahead.

He called Betty to share this snippet of news, re-lit his pipe and smiled. A lengthy pause and Betty returned to the kitchen. 'I was wondering...' I said, faltered and decided to add nothing more. But AW told me to continue, perhaps expecting more good financial news. Deep breath. 'I was thinking... wouldn't it be good if we could perhaps visit Haystacks'? I thought the word 'visit' was appropriate and would keep the practical details of how we would get a 78-year-old man with failing eyesight to the summit. The film crew weren't much better equipped for the ascent with their ridiculously heavy tripod, cumbersome camera and many rolls of film, but there was no easier option.

I had been thinking about this problem for weeks and, whichever way I looked at it, it was clearly a major expedition. It would not be something to undertake on a *Coronation Street* evening. AW's favoured ascents were from Gatesgarth going by Scarth Gap or, alternatively, via Warnscale. Both routes involve around 1500 feet (457 metres) of ascent and a distance of between 1¾ and 2¾ miles (2.8 – 4.4km). Neither, I thought, would be feasible within the confines of a day that had to take travelling time and stops for filming into account. I also knew from our ascent of Pen-y-ghent that progress would necessarily be slow.

Whilst I was thinking of the obstacles to be overcome, AW was silent. Then he called Betty through from the kitchen, 'Richard thinks we should go up Haystacks...' And that, I thought, would be the end of the conversation. Not for the first time I was wrong. As always Betty was key, balancing my desire for what would look good on camera, with a concern not only for her husband's welfare but also for what might please him. I was expecting a straightforward 'no', but, after thinking for a moment, Betty replied: 'That could be interesting. Would you like to do that Red?' Now the real work had to begin...

One way to have taken AW to the summit of Haystacks would have been by helicopter. Getting permission to take off and land might have been tricky, but I am sure we could have arranged it. Looking back now, it seems an obvious solution. In 1985 it was something I did not entertain. It seemed like cheating to arrive at a summit without undertaking any effort to get there. I was also concerned about how AW would cope with a new experience having not even been in a plane before. Helicopters are another challenge and can be very disorientating with their noise, susceptibility to air currents (with sudden, unpredictable buffeting) and the confusion that comes from flying in tight circles. There is another drawback to this mode of travel; the wind speeds need to be low; visibility good and you need to ensure that once you have landed, changing weather does not make a subsequent takeoff impossible. Eric Robson also has an aversion to trusting his life to a 'tin can full of inflammable fuel'. As it turned out my solution proved little better. I suspect Eric had a hand in suggesting it would be an ideal arrangement. Experience has, somewhat belatedly, taught me to be careful when Eric makes a suggestion: there are never any practical difficulties; it seems such a natural idea, you immediately gain an inferiority complex for not having thought about it yourself, and Eric's winsome smile and naturally optimistic outlook on life (flying excepted) mean a tide of positive thinking sweeps everything before it. Eric's solutions are always foolproof: they start with 'nothing can go wrong Richard... just think about it' and end simply... '...and mine's a pint'.

To Eric it's a job well done, but for me it is normally the start of a nightmare. More than once I have embarked on a project buoyed up by much wishful thinking on Eric's part. 'Of course, I've done this before you know...'. If only...

The Eric solution? So simple it was obvious. Hire a tracked vehicle and driver; use it to take AW to the top of the old mine road from Honister Quarry and shorten the actual walking to a mere hop and skip from west of Dubs Quarry, around Black Beck Tarn and the job was as good as done. Thank you, Eric. After many phone calls and a prolonged search through the Yellow Pages, I located a man at Tebay, just off the M6, who owned the requisite machine. He was happy to help and a deal was struck. Thirty years later I would be far more cautious; risk assessments would need to be completed and alternatives considered. In 1985 we simply chose a day, packed our rucksacks and set off for the quarry. And then the reality began to sink in.

The week's filming had been dogged by consistently poor weather: Borrowdale had been awash with water and at Seatoller we had been reduced to filming underneath a bus shelter that failed to live up to its name. The forecast continued to be pessimistic. So on the day we chose for our ascent of Haystacks, it was no surprise when low clouds and grey skies announced that it would not be the ideal early autumn day. I took the crew up the old mine road in the Land Rover and at Dubs Quarry we disembarked. From here we would walk. The three-person film crew somehow managed all of their bulky equipment while I and Production Assistant, Julie Scott, carried food, flasks and an assortment of odds and ends. Betty accompanied us and we waited for the tracked vehicle carrying AW and Eric to appear.

Then I saw it... slowly, very noisily and with absolutely no suspension it clattered, clanged and bumped its way upwards. Progress was at a snail's pace. I could see Eric and AW both wobbling in the cab like a jelly when the mould has just been removed. My original idea was based on an assumption that a tracked vehicle would be able to get further than the Land Rover but when one of the tracks parted company from the complicated mechanism that held it in place, I knew we would all be walking from now on. Eric emerged from the now immobile vehicle declaring it had been a wonderful experience. AW was less convinced.

Normally it is a brisk walk to Haystacks, contouring round to Innominate Tarn before the final, easy ascent onto the summit. That day progress was predictably slow: AW was carefully checking where he put his feet and although Betty, myself and Eric all helped, he did much of the ascent unaided. Almost as soon as we started, the rain

Whilst I fretted about the consistent rain and AW's well-being, and asked for the umpteenth time if he was alright, our star was more concerned about whether the all-important matches were damp, before adding that there was nowhere else he would rather be.

began. Anyone who has walked in the Lakes will know the kind of rain I'm talking about: consistent, increasing in ferocity and, as an upward glance immediately confirmed, settling in for the day. Just walking in this kind of weather with AW would have been an incredible achievement but we were also attempting to film. Every scene we shot was a trial - a logistical challenge of working out how long we could afford to spend on it; checking that AW was as comfortable as possible as we set up the camera; working out how long it would take us to reach our goal and, somewhere at the back of my mind, hoping we would be able to get back down again without anyone becoming hypothermic or, most embarrassingly of all, the need to call out the local mountain rescue team.

We should have been a miserable party but we weren't. Our cameraman John Warwick was not, by any stretch of the imagination, a mountain person (although I did discover in Teesdale he was very knowledgeable about wild orchids). On paper John was not an obvious choice for such a project but he had filmed the original interview with AW in Kendal Green and the pair had got on well. The more unusual an individual, the more John was inclined to like them. Wainwright was John's ideal subject – one you had to work with to get results and where you needed a wide repertoire of skills that involved adopting a variety of unconventional methods. There was another key element also at work that day, although none of us wanted to articulate it. We all knew how much this journey meant to AW. Today would be his last time on Haystacks and we needed to capture the importance and emotion of that final journey. The consistent rain, driven by a steady westerly wind, only added to the atmosphere. Familiar views had to be conjured up out of the imagination. In earlier years, AW would probably have waited for better weather, but we didn't have that option.

What we filmed on Haystacks became just under nine minutes in the final programme, but it is one of the most evocative days filming I have ever undertaken. The dramatic views you get on a good day were flattened in the mist and rain; we didn't have time to explore the jumbled landscape of grass and rocks around the summit or investigate the many hidden corners of this fell, but that did not matter. In decent weather, this mountain has spectacular panoramas – north-east to Fleetwith Pike, east to Grey Knotts and Brandreth, south-east to Green and Great Gable, south to Kirk Fell, south-west to Pillar or west to High Crag and High Stile. In spite of its relatively low height it can still catch the wind and I've had nights there in May with snow in the air. Today more people pass this way than 30 years ago but, after the last walkers have descended in the late afternoon, peace returns to the fell. It has a sombre beauty.

When Wainwright was here in the 1950s the summit was rarely visited and you were unlikely to meet any other walkers. Today that has changed. Even in the atrocious weather we had to contend with, between 20 and 30 other people had ventured out. As Eric and AW approached Green Crag, Eric reminded AW of what he had written at the start of his chapter on the mountain - that memorable phrase describing it, 'like a shaggy terrier in the company of foxhounds' (a beautifully descriptive phrase he also used almost word for word when describing Helm Crag in *The Central Fells*). AW replied, 'I wouldn't change any of that, that's what I think about Haystacks', adding that, 'none of the books on Lakeland ever mentioned Haystacks, or rarely, just in passing. The glossy brochures never mentioned Haystacks'. He accepted that his *Guide* may have contributed to a significant rise in popularity and that many people wrote to him describing their own experiences on the mountain.

AW was tentative where the path was strewn with boulders, but on firm, clear sections he made good progress, surprising, as he strode past, some other walkers who had paused for a lunch in the few moments when the rain had marginally relented. During the ascent Wainwright also spoke about his plans for a last book to be published by the *Westmorland Gazette* – one that would coincide with his 80th birthday and which he was going to call *Ex-Fellwanderer*. And then, finally, we arrived at Innominate Tarn. Wainwright and Eric sheltered on the far side in the lee of a large boulder. The wind was rippling across the tarn and everywhere looked sombre and grey. We were all soaked. The electronic cameras of today have an aversion to any form of damp and would not have coped with the conditions we encountered. They announce their displeasure without warning by simply shutting down and refusing to restart. Traditional film cameras, with their Meccano-like construction, are far more robust - which was just as well as the scene we were capturing would not be repeated.

'I shall end up here…' was how AW began. He was gazing out across the tarn, seeing it as he had many years earlier, with every detail etched in his mind's eye. 'Somebody will carry me up in a little box and leave me by the side.' He then informed us that he would not be alone, because a few months previously a woman had written to him saying her husband had died and wished to have his ashes scattered near this spot. Other people had told him they would join him when their time came. 'So I'll be in company… and several others have written and said when the time comes we'll join you. So I'll be in company… lots of company'. A wry smile spread across AW's face at the thought of being with others in the afterlife – companionship he had studiously avoided in this one. Or perhaps anything that involved Innominate Tarn would be acceptable. 'Could you wish for a better place?' were Wainwright's final words on the subject. A question that required no answer and our final image, beautifully captured by John Warwick, was of AW seated by himself and at peace looking across the water of Innominate Tarn.

Innominate Tarn from near the summit of Haystacks with Great Gable dominating the skyline.

In thinking about AW in the years since his death, it is that day by Innominate Tarn I remember. The tarn has changed over the years since we made that last journey – the water level seems higher and, if anything, the tarn more sombre, even on sunny days. And the memory of AW always haunts me. That wild, wet and windy day on Haystacks was pivotal. A process that had started in the Haweswater Hotel on another wet day was completed on Haystacks. From then on we not only made a series of outstandingly successful films together, but he said I became his eyes and ears into the high places he could not longer visit. This was not the gruff, isolated individual you often hear about, nor was it the predictable person many assume AW to have been. Even so, I recognised that AW had a different relationship with the world around him. Friendship and trust did not come easily to him. They might vanish quickly and, I was convinced, were not the result of a conscious action on his part but a deep-seated part of his make-up.

The journey back down to Honister quarry was only marginally easier than the ascent. In the hours we had spent getting to and around Innominate Tarn, the broken track from our vehicle had been reunited with the body and our all-terrain machine was once again all-terrain, although no less uncomfortable. It was a damp team and a very wet camera that returned to the hotel that evening, but we all knew that the images we had captured were worth the effort.

It was the final day of filming and we could not believe our luck. The conversation over dinner revolved around Wainwright, who had shown us all that the determination that characterises the *Guide* was undiminished. Having agreed to visit Innominate Tarn one last time, he had displayed a resilience that was inspirational. The team were changed and dry and the camera and recording equipment were left to air naturally in various rooms and, hopefully, would be none the worse for their experience. My thoughts, though, were elsewhere. Over the last six months I had seen AW begin to embrace the filming process and to enjoy the company of what I thought of as our little anarchic band. We were seven very different people (I always included Betty as part of the team), yet somehow, with a fair measure of luck, we had completed five distinctive films that reflected Wainwright's love of northern England. Now the long process of film-making would move indoors and I could relax a little as we began editing in earnest.

Wider Horizons

AW always had a capacity to surprise. For a man who had never left Britain, and who did not like an exposed mountain ridge, he had a substantial collection of mountaineering books from around the world. Notable amongst them were three volumes of *The Mountain World* dating from the 1950s and 60s. They were originally published by the Swiss Foundation for Alpine Research (with the English translation courtesy of Allen & Unwin) and they gave the man for whom Everest was 'a pipe dream', up-to-date accounts of worldwide mountaineering activity. Wainwright's reading included a new perspective on the first ascent of the Matterhorn, the latest developments in the Hindu Kush, Baffin Island, the Karakoram and Alaska. Among the pieces he read were articles on the training of Sherpas and place names in Baltistan.

One day, when we were talking about high altitude climbing and the recent deaths of Joe Tasker and Peter Boardman on Everest, AW expressed some disappointment about never visiting any of the higher mountain ranges. 'Not that I would have had the time or money and I certainly don't regret what I've done here... I wouldn't have wanted to miss any of that'. Sensing a genuine disappointment, I asked, 'Would you like to go to the Alps?'.

'What do you mean?'

'Well... we could go there', I suggested, not having the slightest idea of how we would do it but thinking it might be possible. Wainwright considered this for a long time. We even discussed the logistics and how we would arrange a trip to Chamonix. I said I had been there and was sure he would be impressed. Eventually AW answered: 'I don't think so. It's a bit late now. Anyway... we've got Scotland to explore. And you'll like that. There's no better sight than travelling over Rannoch Moor in the setting sun'.

Nonetheless, I sensed real disappointment in AW's voice and wished he and I had met some years earlier.

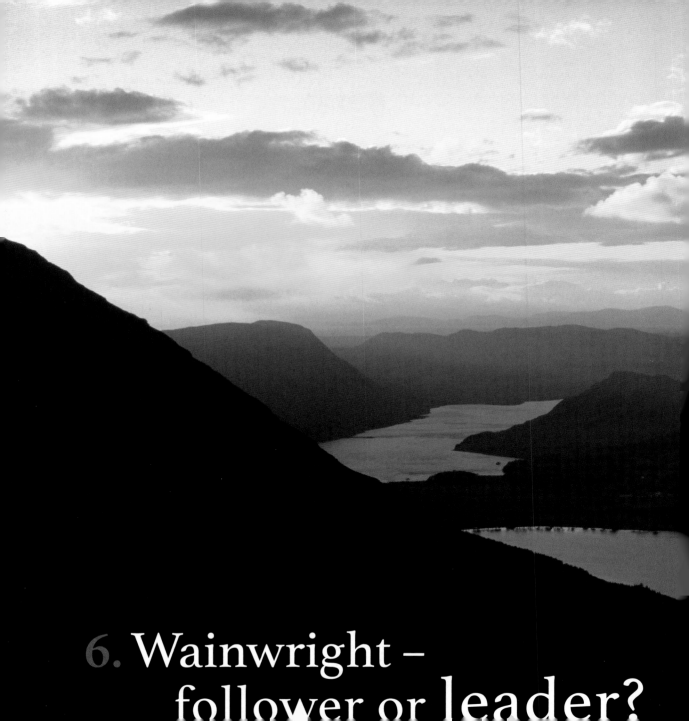

6. Wainwright –
follower or leader?

Whatever measure you might choose to take, it would be hard to find another British guidebook writer who stands comparison with Wainwright. There is not only the wealth of detail to be found in his major works but the way this is shaped and moulded into a coherent whole. In each book there is a delicate balance to be found, both in the chapters and within individual pages and this applies to both illustrations and text. Additionally there is Wainwright himself. His voice gains in confidence in successive books, sharing detailed knowledge, a wide variety of opinions and, let's be honest, a fair number of prejudices. It is also clear that AW is a diligent author, someone who has expended endless boot leather tramping and re-tramping the ground checking every aspect of the landscape. Driving all this is an unwavering sense of purpose, of a job to be done and a mission to be accomplished. The smaller format books are also works of great beauty, especially the early editions with their rounded corners and better quality paper. If we think about Wainwright's achievement, these are all significant elements but they do beg one important question. It is a question raised by Nicholas T. Parsons in his thorough, scholarly history of guidebooks, *Worth the Detour*. Put at its most simple, 'What are guidebooks for?'

I had thought of the history of the guidebook in terms of Defoe, Ruskin and Wordsworth. A history of the Grand Tour, of Baedeker, of the Ward Lock *Red Guides*, Baddeley's *Thorough Guides* and, in a related field, Sir Nikolaus Pevsner's *The Buildings of England* or Sir John Betjeman's *Shell Guides*. Thinking specifically about walking and climbing we have the excellent Scottish Mountaineering Club guides; the work of F. S. Smythe in the first half of the 20th century, and later, among many others, the photographer and writer Walter Poucher. Of course, there seem endless books

Today most routes and rights of way are clearly signed, but earlier travellers relied on an ever expanding range of guidebooks to find their way into the hills. These works spawned an industry that continues unabated to this day. Whilst useful, there is a danger of placing too much emphasis on them and losing our sense of genuine adventure. Over 40 years after Wainwright devised his Coast to Coast route, I am pleased that not all of it, as here near Keld, has been signed.

of the *Fifty Best...* or *One Hundred Best...* variety, and some of them none the worse for that approach. There are companies who have founded their whole business on guidebook publication and other guides that are not the work of a single individual but a team effort. Recently there have been what some call 'anti guidebooks' with comments suggesting you would be silly to linger in a particular place or that another has no merit other than that it is easy to leave. Nevertheless, it came as something of surprise to discover, thanks to Nicholas T. Parsons' endeavours, that the guidebook, as a genre, has a lineage that stretches back some 18 centuries. In essence his work is a guidebook to Guidebooks. But this is only part of his achievement, for this detailed scholarly work is clearly, like Wainwright's books, a labour of love.

One of the paradoxes is whether such works serve to make us walkers and hillgoers more independent by providing information that enables us to make informed choices or if, on the other hand, they serve, in Parsons' phrase, as a 'white stick' which many of us slavishly follow. Investigating where Wainwright fits into this tradition is useful, for it allows us to understand not only his success, but more importantly, his achievement.

Early writers, such as the prolific Daniel Defoe, were less than complimentary about the Lake District. I first read his epic *A Tour Through the Whole Island of Great Britain* in the 1970s. It was published in three volumes between 1724 and 1727 and he is often thought of as an important authority on early 18th century England. The book is not a guidebook in the modern sense of the word but a rich, multi-faceted document that reflects Defoe's experience as a journalist, spy, businessman and much more besides. But Defoe struggled to comprehend the high places. The hills of the southern Lake District were not only formidable, 'but they had a kind of unhospitable terror in them', and when he entered Westmorland he found it, 'a country eminent only for being the wildest, most barren and frightful of any that I have passed over in England... the west side, which borders Cumberland, is indeed bounded by a chain of almost unpassable mountains, which, in the language of the country, are called Fells...' While Defoe published his *Tour* towards the end of his life (he died in 1731), it wasn't long before writers began to appreciate the wilder and 'unhospitable' characteristics of the Lake District. Today we can view Defoe as looking backwards to a previous age, while Thomas West, a Jesuit priest, was one of the first to appreciate and articulate a Romantic vision of this landscape.

Like Wainwright, West had a master plan and ordered his book *A Guide to the Lakes*, which was first published in 1778, around 12 principal Lakes. These were selected not solely on their intrinsic merit but also for the ease which with it was possible to visit them. His guide was aimed at artists (especially those concerned with the landscape) as much as tourists and he included viewpoints (often called 'stations') from which the aesthetic qualities of the landscape could be understood and appreciated. But it is what West says about Lakeland's high places that are most revealing. Here is part of his account of travelling from Keswick to Buttermere via the Newlands valley. I have tried to remain faithful to West's writing, altering the spelling, but not the place names, to modern norms.

'Company who visit the Vale of Keswick, and view its lake from Castlerigg , Latrigg and Swinside, and the vicarage, imagine inaccessible mountains only remain beyond the line of this amazing tract. But whoever takes a ride up Newland vale, will be agreeably surprised with some of the finest solemn pastoral scenes, they have yet beheld. Here present themselves an arrangement of vast mountains, entirely new, both in form and colouring of rock; large hollow craters scooped in their bosoms, once the seeming seats of raging liquid fire, though at present overflowing with the purest water, that foams down the craggy brows; other woods ornamental their base, and other lakes clear as the Derwent, lie at their feet...

'Above Gasgadale [possibly where today's Keskadale farm is situated], the last houses in Newland, no traces of human industry appear. All is naked solitude and simple nature... Whoever would enjoy, with ease and safety, Alpine views, and pastoral scenes in the sublime style, may have them in this morning ride... It will not be labour lost to walk a few roods here, and see a new creation of mountains, as unlike those left behind, as the Andes are to the Alps.

'Descend the tract on the left, and you soon have in sight the highest possible contrast in nature. For spiral towering mountains, dark, dun, and gloomy at noon-day, rise immediately from the western extremity of the deep narrow Dell and hang over Buttermere. The most southern is by the dalesmen, from its form, called Hay-rick; the most pyramidal, High-crag; the third High-style; and the fourth Red-pike.

'There is one curious spectacle often seen by the shepherd, on the tops of these mountains, which the traveller may never chance to see...What I mean is, the effect of mists, which frequently involve every object round the bases of these eminences, and which, in the district of pointed hills just described, must be experienced in the greatest perfection.'

This may be the first mention of AW's beloved Haystacks in literature and to me it seems clear that West knew this landscape as well as any of his contemporaries. Indeed, he chides the poet Thomas Gray who, in one of his letters, indulged in what West thought was a fanciful description of Borrowdale. There was, West argued, none of the dangers in travelling through Borrowdale that you might find in crossing the Alps or the Italian Appenines [today more usually called the Apennines]. And to ram the point home, West declares that, 'no villainous banditti haunt the mountains; innocent people live in the dells. Every cottager is narrative of all he knows; and mountain virtue, and pastoral hospitality are found at every farm'.

The Grand Tour had been popular since the latter part of the 17th century and, tapping into this, West's book was influential, suggesting as it did that there were majestic sights to be seen nearer home and equally powerful experiences. It also shows that from this relatively early time authors were not content to simply describe the landscape but felt impelled to express their opinion about it. Of course, we can find such opinions throughout all of AW's work and he becomes less cautious about expressing them as his *Guide* progresses.

As I started working with AW on the films, I spent a long time annotating his books, trying to analyse what made them so distinctive. It was a harder task than I first imagined, but it soon became clear that Wainwright was familiar with many of his predecessors. And like AW, West's work shows that these early guidebook writers had both an eloquent prose style and, for their time, a detailed knowledge of the landscape.

Baddeley's *English Lake District*, first published in 1880, was the most famous work in his *Thorough Guide* series. He takes a broadly alphabetical approach (one that was still followed in later editions) and uses the principal settlements as his starting point. This is standard fare for a tourist guide, but there's more to Baddeley than just a description of the Lakes' main attractions. He is enthusiastic about its fells and mountains: 'There are not,' he says, 'perhaps, in the kingdom, two mountains more thoroughly pleasing to the eye than the Lancashire fells of the Old Man and Wetherlam'. More surprisingly for a guidebook writer Baddeley (probably influenced by his contemporary John Ruskin) makes a strong call for the preservation of Lakeland and while not against all industry, argues, 'A single mine may ruin a whole valley', adding, 'Half a dozen of the same sort as the one which has despoiled Glenridding of its glory and polluted the surface of Ullswater, would ruin the district'.

Baddeley, like most writers, is a product of his age, one where the cost of travel, meals and accommodation together with suggestions for 14-day tours from different centres are compulsory information for the traveller. The guide has a number of Bartholomew maps, but it is Baddeley's confident voice, no doubt shaped by his experience of teaching, that comes through loud and clear. When he talks of the 'reckless vandalism' of some visitors, his comments are echoed directly by Wainwright in his *Personal Notes in Conclusion* to *The Southern Fells*, the Ullscarf chapter in *The Central Fells*, and the pages on Blencathra in *The Northern Fells*, to give just a few examples.

Yet Baddeley's landscape is one to be appreciated predominantly from a distance in the manner of the Grand Tour. Entering Great Langdale from the south is an opportunity for Baddeley to enthuse about the view, but it is the general panorama that interests him, not the individual details that every fellwalker recalls after a magnificent day on the hills. 'As we climb, the "Lions" of Langdale pop up over the intervening pass with striking suddenness and boldness of contour. In the way of surprises there is, perhaps, nothing equal to this in the district, unless it be Honister Crag at the moment of gaining the top of Borrowdale Hause…. Where else, it may well be asked, do 2,500 feet create such an impression on the mind of the beholder?' Baddeley has an affinity with this landscape that is anything but superficial. For example, he gives us this vivid description of the Jaws of Borrowdale: 'Here is a wonderful richness of rock-colouring,

No guidebook can really anticipate those magical few seconds when an otherwise undistinguished day is suddenly transformed by a shaft of light, or the passing of a quick rain shower. The moment when you look up from the way immediately ahead and see a landscape that quite literally takes your breath away.

at no time of the year so striking as in mid-winter, when the combined tints of the dead bracken, the oak coppices and the lofty crags, diffuse a glow through the atmosphere which often colours even the faces of those who walk between them.'

Many of Baddeley's original words survive unaltered in later copies, including my 15th edition, which probably dates from the 1920s, and was published over a decade after his death. In spite of the tourist boom following Wordsworth and other writers, some descriptions, such as the journey from Wasdale to Buttermere via Black Sail Pass and Scarth Gap, are little altered from what West wrote over 100 years earlier. Later editions include panoramas like the view from Orrest Head and from Helvellyn, whilst the first edition only had topographical maps and a sketch map showing the routes over Esk Hause. Half a century or so later Wainwright would bring a precision and detail to describing Lakeland. However, he was able to draw on the work of these earlier authors, so he is both part of a tradition but developed it in a new and imaginative way.

When there was a break from filming AW often spoke about how he had produced his books. It was clear that he respected earlier guidebook writers, yet he always checked everything against the OS maps, using both the 1:25,000 series and even larger scale ones when necessary.

From West's time onwards there is no shortage of writers prepared to expound the merits of the Lake District. Herman Prior's *Guide to the Lake District of England* was published in the latter part of the 19th century and was soon reprinted in a pocket sized version. Prior's work predates Baddeley, yet it appears strikingly modern in many respects and for someone born in Surrey and who came to guidebook writing later in life, having been a barrister and novelist, he is surprisingly knowledgeable about the Lake District and its mountains. Here we find a writer giving the total time required to complete a route based on 3 mph for road walking on 'ordinary ground' and 1½ mph for mountainous terrain. Prior also devotes a section of his book specifically to the Mountains and had clearly thought about what his readers might require: 'In the original edition of this work, the author deemed it desirable to notice popular ascents only. The complete orthodox list, may, however, be of use to the stranger, if only preventing him from wasting time and labour on second and third-class results'. For a modern reader it is somewhat confusing, and perhaps artificial, that Prior divides his book into *Pedestrian Routes* and *Mountains*, but his level of detail is impressive.

Looking again at the popular route from Buttermere to Wasdale via Black Sail, there is a precision in Prior's description that other writers lack. It is, according to Prior, 34 minutes from Buttermere Church to the head of the lake. This is walking to a detailed timetable. Likewise, when the reader is taken up High Crag to Scarth Gap he is given explicit instructions. 'Follow the zigzags up the grass shoulder, having the wall on your left for 10 minutes from the bridge, when the track goes through a gate in it, and then bears left, having another (broken) wall on its right, for 9 minutes; it then quits the wall, and, in 8 minutes, reaches a plateau, where it runs level for 2 minutes in the direction of the last wall (S) and then begins to ascend again.

In 3 minutes further, you go through a gate, and keep the same direction (S) for 9 minutes further, after which the track bears left (SE) and in 1½ minutes reaches the edge of the grass and rock plateau which forms the summit of Scarth Gap'.

It is hard to imagine a more comprehensive description for a Victorian pedestrian with an accurate pocket watch and a disciplined step! However, his attitude to describing the more precise aspects of mountain ascents is more ambivalent. 'No description or details are given in any of the Mountain Ascents. To the tourist who does not know the country such detail is a mere catalogue of names: to one who does it is superfluous. In either case, however, a good map and pocket compass will be all-sufficient to determine the name of any particular summit'. Prior seems intent on following his own advice when mentioning Pike o'Blisco which stands proud and is a distinctive feature of the skyline when seen from the valley floor in Great Langdale. AW has nothing but praise for the noble Pike, yet Herman Prior can dismiss it in a mere six lines. For once, he fails to capture any of the magic of this fine hill:

'Overshadows Blea Tarn, at the head of the Langdales. It is most easily ascended from the Wrynose Pass, and thence by the pool called Red Tarn; but can also be "done" by Oxendale, at the head of Great Langdale, in connection with Brow Fell and Crinkle Crags... The view from the summit is good in the Langdale and Windermere direction.'

This description could hardly be more prosaic, yet it is a different story when it comes to Pillar Rock. I am sure Prior is reflecting the Victorian fascination with it and uppermost in his mind would have been the two fatalities that had already occurred there. Today there are around 100 routes on this prominent face, but in 1872 only four climbing routes had been pioneered on the rock, following the first ascent in 1826. Prior's description is precise and accompanied by a detailed drawing. He takes the timid explorer who baulks at the prospect where 'the slightest slip would be instantly fatal', right onto the face: 'A climb of about 10 feet out of this gill places you on the edge of a grassy platform, sloping steeply from the foot of the cliff on the left, to the brow of the precipice on the right. The farther side of this is denuded to a smooth slab of slate, about 30 feet long, and 5 feet wide, inclined athwart the route. Across it, a few feet from its lower edge, runs a shallow horizontal crack filled with grass and moss. By means of this the slab can be traversed safely by one sure of his footing, who can trust his head until he lands on a little sloping shelf, not larger than the seat of the chair...'

For those of us who see this as a deterrent rather than an enticement, Prior has these words of advice, 'The descent will be found to be neither more difficult nor more dangerous than the ascent. It would hardly be right to suppress a word of warning to would-be climbers who may be tempted, without sufficient qualifications, to essay this, the most hazardous of the two or three risky ascents in the District. Only a good cragsman ought to attempt the feat; for he who scales the Pillar Rock literally carries his life in his hand...' This was advice AW had no trouble following.

By the end of the 19th century there was a proliferation of Lakeland guidebooks, with each claiming to have its own, distinct quality. By the time Canon Hardwicke Rawnsley and Thomas Bakewell came to revise *Jenkinson's Practical Guide to the English Lake District*, it featured detailed, if crudely drawn, fold-out panoramic views from Skiddaw and Scafell Pike.

These historical guidebooks mirror the growth in walking and by 1863 we find *A Guide to the English Lake District* with the sub-heading *Intended Principally for the Use of Pedestrians*. The author, *A Cambridge Man*, makes his intentions clear from the outset: 'The chief object of this Guidebook is different to that of its numerous predecessors. It is intended to be... a *pedestrians'* guide, and hence many mountains and mountain-walks are described or noticed in it which other books have altogether omitted.' For what I think is the first time, the author chose to concentrate on mountain routes and that other staple fare of previous books, 'towns and much-frequented places', are only briefly mentioned. The author is dismissive of the need to hire someone as a guide provided an early start is made and the walker has built up his knowledge on easier mountains and passes. He is at pains to set his readers at ease. 'Much is said of the danger of mists and the horror of a night on the mountain: mists, no doubt are unpleasant, and may cause delay, but it does not of necessity follow, as some people seem to think, that a man, because he is in a mist, must fall down a precipice.'

The start of my own journey with AW. These two early edition books – The Eastern Fells and Far Eastern Fells – began my exploration of Wainwright as both a writer and a person. Even in 1976 I was surprised that no one appeared to have explored their literary merit. The often expressed view was that they were impressive books but of only local significance.

Nicholas T. Parsons makes the important point that guidebooks can serve as a barometer of taste and through them we can see how those tastes change through the years. However, although there are notable exceptions, relatively few guidebooks set out to deliberately change attitudes. Indeed, looking at just a sample of the enormous amount of such books about the Lake District, there is a monotonous, repetitive quality about many of them. So the obvious question is: where does Wainwright fit into this tradition of guidebook writing? If we accept that his work is not simply a phenomenal achievement on his part but has exceptional qualities, what makes his *Guide* so enduring and important?

On holiday with AW and Betty in the west of Scotland, autumn 1984. Spending days and weeks with AW allowed me to observe his relationship with the landscape; his ability to recall minute details from 30 or 40 years previously and to see how he planned his books. Even with his extremely poor eyesight he still took copious photographs, continuing a habit he had established from his earliest walks.

Shaken, never stirred

Being driven by Betty was always... how shall I put this... an energising experience, and certainly not one for the timid. Her pale lilac Nissan Micra was only 12½ feet long and a tad over five feet high, but in Betty's hands it always felt much larger than that. AW would sit in the passenger seat contentedly puffing away, seemingly totally oblivious to the car's haphazard progress along the road with what, from my position, seemed a succession of near misses.

Betty was also a timid passenger in my Land Rover, especially when it was taken off-road. This was not helped by Eric's assertion that his Citroen DS, with its self-levelling suspension, would be able to mimic everything a Land Rover could do but with far more panache and finesse. Although Eric – never one to easily admit he might be wrong – did become somewhat muted as we forded the River Rawthey north of Sedbergh on our way to Cautley Spout in the Howgills. The water was halfway up the doors and rising. 'Try doing that in a Citroen' I said, but Eric was temporarily deaf.

These examples of what a Land Rover can achieve did not impress Betty either. 'Do we really have to do this', she said later that day as we traversed a rough slope at a 45 degree angle. My suggestion that if we all leant to the right, it might prevent the vehicle somersaulting down the hill was likewise not appreciated.

There was a paradox here too, for the more difficult it was becoming to reach the places that inspired Wainwright, the more he valued my ability to negotiate access for our 12-seater vehicle. Eric and the crew grumbled about the lack of space inside (especially with all the filming paraphernalia) and Betty was always concerned we would meet our maker.

With the help of farmers, landowners, factors, gamekeepers, stalkers, ghillies and many others we were able to use tracks to access not just the Howgill Fells, but areas of Swaledale, the Pennines, Lakeland, the North York Moors and vast swathes of Scotland. But there was one example where I completely failed to reassure Betty. During our filming in the Cairngorms we drove up the long winding track almost to the head of Loch Einich. At one point there is a steep zigzag turn that ruffled her composure. 'Richard, one slip here and we'll all be dead', came a frantic shout from the back. There was silence until AW, a few moments later, joined in: 'If I'd have known we could do this, I would never have walked anywhere'.

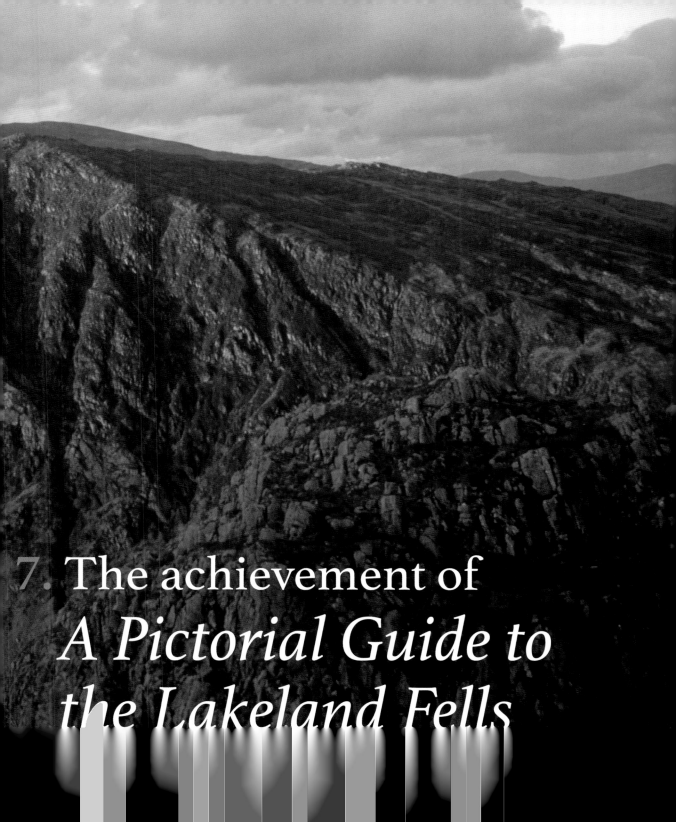

7. The achievement of
*A Pictorial Guide to
the Lakeland Fells*

The achievement of A Pictorial Guide to the Lakeland Fells. Late evening light on Fleetwith Pike. Over 30 years later I find it strange to undertake walks in Lakeland and not have to recount my exploits to AW. A general description was not acceptable: I needed to be absolutely precise in my route description and provide information about any changes I had noticed. Wainwright always remembered, with absolute clarity, his own visits when working on the Guide.

Today we open any part of AW's seven-volume *Guide* and are presented with the totality of his work. The result is so impressive that it is hard to step back and see the individual components. Certain elements fit within the tradition of guidebook writing, while others are a development of it. These include a distinctive voice – one that has definite preferences; one that knows what information is useful to, and expected by, the reader and one who is clearly knowledgeable about his subject. I would argue that Wainwright does even more than this and moves the guidebook tradition into wholly new territory.

Compared with his predecessors, Wainwright had a novel way of defining Lakeland, dividing it into sections by using natural boundaries. These form the basis of the individual volumes. This, as AW himself said, wasn't perfect. As he also pointed out, any division has a somewhat arbitrary nature to it. I am not the first to note that the southern volume is quite problematic, but most walkers would think he did a pretty good job overall. However, his concentration on the high ground does mean that some fells that perhaps merited inclusion are left out. Hence the subsequent volume *The Outlying Fells of Lakeland*, with its somewhat misleading title and odd rationale. An author with a less rigid approach would have found space for Orrest Head within the original work and not excluded it simply because of its height. Surely there is more to say about Orrest Head than Arnison Crag, which is the first fell featured in the *Guide*. By any standards this isn't the strongest start and AW seems a victim of his own prescriptive approach. I would argue that it is not until the Catstycam chapter that AW really gets into his stride. Here is the Wainwright I knew: a man full of enthusiasm, passion, knowledge and a deep, abiding love of the fells.

One of the many ways I remember AW – looking out over a landscape he could no longer see clearly, but with his inner eye as sharp and questioning as ever. Betty had also been hard at work – this is the smartest I ever saw AW. Within days the inevitable burn marks and holes would appear!

No guidebook is perfect and this is evident at the start of *The Eastern Fells* where a right-hand page lists the fells in alphabetical order, while the map on the adjoining page numbers them by height. The map on the back dust jacket is much easier to follow, with its listing of fells by altitude. By book 3, *The Central Fells*, this had become the norm. And as I mentioned at the beginning of this book, following a route from one peak to another can involve frantic moving from one chapter to another and even from book to book. Yet, for hundreds of thousands of readers right across Britain and beyond, Wainwright's achievements far outweigh any criticism. The big question is: why have his books become such an unrivalled success? Why do they still appeal to both hardy fellwalkers and those who prefer to enjoy Lakeland from the comfort of an armchair?

Before I first met AW in 1982, I set about reading and re-reading the Lakeland *Guide* in earnest. To use a modern term, I wanted to 'reverse engineer' the *Guide* to understand how it worked, and, more importantly from my perspective, what motivated the man who wrote it. Here was an author who, although conscious of the guidebook tradition, had approached this genre in an entirely new way. Permeating every aspect of his work is the need for order. At the end of *The Western Fells* there's more evidence of this as Wainwright reveals the list of his six best fells and summits. As if sensing such lists might be controversial, he seeks to avoid the inevitable readers' letters by also including his finest ridge walks and, more vaguely, the 'best places for a fellwalker to be'. Given AW's love of such lists, I'll follow suit, so here are my top six reasons of why I think the *Guide* is exceptional and what sets it apart from all those works that preceded it. Why, in short, it is a literary masterpiece. They are:

1. His *vision*
2. The *structural unity* that underpins the whole work
3. The *quality* of the work and the *detail* it contains
4. *Research* that goes far beyond what is required for a guidebook
5. Wainwright's idiosyncratic *humour* together with his sense of mischief
6. A *strong authorial voice*.

Firstly, and arguably most importantly, there is the wonderful *vision* that underpins each volume and forms a backbone to the whole work. It can be seen throughout and begins with that division of Lakeland into seven separate sectors – areas that make sense from a walker's perspective, rather than, as in many previous works, those that explore Lakeland from the main settlements. Wainwright's approach means, for example, that the tourist 'hot spot' of Windermere is absent. Such an omission would have been unthinkable to previous writers of Lakeland guidebooks.

Another aspect of that overarching vision can be seen on every page which is painstakingly produced by hand and devoid of that staple of guidebook writers – photographs. AW himself said that nothing made by human hand is perfect and in spite of his best efforts, individual pages can be difficult to read. Page 4 of the Rossett Pike chapter in the *Southern Fells* captures the infamous Rossett Gill perfectly and is beautiful to look at, but taken as a body of text that is relieved by one small illustration, it is not easy to read. Thinking on a larger perspective, many readers might judge the *Northern Fells* to be the weakest book in the series, with AW needing more illustrations to flesh out the individual chapters.

Finally, there is Wainwright's enthusiasm for every aspect of natural Lakeland. That enthusiasm is wide-ranging, encompassing the fells, the lakes, becks and tarns, the passes and old roads, the rocky crests, ridges and impressive cliff faces, the dramatic slopes that tumble down to the valley floor, the centuries-old communities, the traditional way of life and much more besides. Which brings me neatly to my second point.

It is this – the *Guide,* whether judged by individual volumes or as a complete body of work, would be immeasurably poorer and far less influential if it wasn't underpinned by such a solid and well executed *structural unity*. Bookending each volume is an introduction to the region and those *Personal Notes*. Those interested in Wainwright minutiae will note how a somewhat messy attempt to show a miniature drawing of each summit noted in the view, such as in pages 9 and 10 of the Dollywaggon Pike chapter in the *Eastern Fells*, was soon dropped.

But let's return to the bigger picture. AW was proud of the way he structured each chapter – the introduction, map, the various lines of ascent, the ridge routes and, concluding each chapter, the summit view. Within that unvarying structure Wainwright allowed himself room to manoeuvre, to add extra drawings as he saw fit and to insert the quirky, sometimes vitriolic asides that became characteristic of his work. So how might we sum up this achievement? I cannot find anyone who has tried to be as comprehensive as AW in describing the Lakeland fells. It surely cannot be an exaggeration to say that, for the first time, an author gives walkers everything they need to know together with quite a lot they may not have realised they needed. Wainwright was fond of using the word 'expedition' and in one way he is absolutely right – the *Guide* gives not only factual information for an expedition, but, much more importantly, an understanding of the landscape, together with its culture and history. Thought about in this way, it is more appropriate to view AW's *magnum opus* not as a guidebook – albeit an exceptionally good one – but as something altogether more important.

It is, I would suggest, a natural human interest to want to document our surroundings. We can see this in the drawings left by early cave dwellers around 13,000-14,000 years ago in Creswell Crags in north-east Derbyshire, close to the border with Nottinghamshire. Much later, early in the 12th century, that impulse can be seen in a different way, when a group of Dominican monks began a Concordance to the Bible. At first this was a verbal record noting where words had occurred.

A little over two centuries later it became a written work and by the sixteenth century there was an English version, albeit only to the New Testament. Today, sitting alongside these works, although not strictly a Concordance, are a number of Biblical Commentaries. With an emphasis on recent scholarship, these works seek to explain and aid an understanding of the Bible. And in terms of the Lake District, this is how we can best appreciate AW's work. It is, I would claim, both a Concordance and Commentary of the place he loved beyond all others and one which shaped his adult life. However, having an ambition to produce a great work is one thing; actually achieving it is another. Which brings us to my third point.

Taken as a whole, and with one or two minor exceptions, one aspect of AW's *Guide* is immediately clear, even on a cursory reading. It is not simply the imaginative counterpointing of text, illustrations and maps but the sheer *detail* and *quality* of the work. It's easy to prove this. Just try, for example, to copy – and copying is so much easier than origination – the map and text that show the summits of Harrison Stickle and Pike How bestriding pages 5 and 6 of that chapter in *The Central Fells*. Or if you are keen for a more demanding challenge, flip a few pages forward in the same book and attempt Helm Crag, again pages 5 and 6.

Sitting in his Kendal living room, with a steady stream of smoke snaking upwards from his pipe and with his favourite cat Totty moving from his lap to the top of the chair, round behind his head and returning to his lap, AW spoke at length about how he had completed his mammoth project. He talked about how he discarded early drafts because the text on the right hand side was, to use printers' jargon, ragged and not justified. I said that must have been incredibly frustrating having put so much effort into the original work over many evenings. Evenings that soon stretched into months. 'No', was his reply, 'I wanted it to be as perfect as possible'. Aiming for that perfection led, as Hunter Davies has noted, to the self-imposed rule of not splitting a word or using a hyphen. 'Once I had seen how messy it looked, I had no option', was the reason he started all over again.

There was much more to Wainwright's achievement than is often realised. He devised his own legend for the maps, differentiating between routes that could be followed in bad visibility and those he thought would give problems. He decided to show the difference between a wall that was intact and one that was broken. Likewise with fences. Motivating him was the need to show the ground in a way that was helpful to fellow walkers and that they would recognise. Again to use printers' terminology, he utilised different font sizes and found a way to mimic the effect of bold and italic type.

AW's Coast to Coast route near Orton after a late snowfall, with the Howgill Fells in the distance. It is a fascinating exercise to take a photograph of a landscape that AW depicted and then compare it to his work. I think there are few better ways of appreciating his achievement in producing his guidebooks.

The illustrations and maps are no less fascinating. He used both the 2½ and 6-inch OS maps and sometimes even larger scale ones. Significantly, he not only checked his work against the OS but also theirs against his. While expressing admiration for the work and commitment of the surveyors (and dedicating Book One of the *Guide* to them), he was not above chastising them for the errors he discovered. On page 4 of Scoat Fell (*Western Fells*) he is highly critical of the OS, saying their contours are 'grossly inaccurate and misleading'. As an aside, if you are reading the revised second edition you might wonder if I have quoted AW correctly. Unfortunately, these 'revised editions' are not limited to showing current routes of ascent but have altered the text in places, and such changes are unannounced.

If final proof of Wainwright's obsessive pursuit of detail and quality is needed, why not look at one of my favourite Lakeland spots, St Sunday Crag above Patterdale. Study, for a minute or two, page 5 in that chapter in *The Eastern Fells* and now close the book. Imagine constructing that page using the OS maps of the time, the photographs you took on location (where AW's images were more an aide memoire than anything else) and your field notes. In recent years there's been an interest in AW trivia, so I'll add a little to that too. Here's another challenge: using pages 3 and 4 from the Blake Fell chapter in *The Western Fells*, and either by copying or counting, give an *exact* figure for the number of pen strokes AW used to make those two pages. That, in a nutshell, shows his achievement. I did ask AW a similar question and, on this rare occasion, he was stumped for an answer. Somewhat flummoxed, the response was simple, 'I don't know. I've never counted them…', and, as he did quite frequently, he changed the subject.

It is my argument that the *Pictorial Guide* is an important work of genuine literary merit and a milestone spanning genres that include guidebook, outdoor and the more loosely defined nature writing. Like all such work it has its high and low points. What makes AW's work unusual is that most of it is of an exceptionally high standard, so when some pages fall short of the very best, they tend to stand out. A good example is the small text used extensively on page 6 of the Helm Crag chapter in *The Central Fells*. What AW is saying is relevant, but there is a basic problem with it. It is not easy to read and appears as one solid block of text which isn't helped by leaving little space between the paragraphs. In a similar vein, page 12 of the High Raise chapter is too crowded for my taste and AW's rigid plan comes unstuck when, just a few pages later, page 7 of High Seat has to accommodate details of an ascent route, a summit description and drawing, together with two ridge routes and a map illustrating them. And it must have been a hugely frustrating moment when Wainwright discovered that the summit map of the Wasdale Red Pike would not fit onto his double page, so the small north extension had to sit untidily at the top of the adjacent page (Red Pike (W) 3 & 4, *Western Fells*). Elsewhere the crowded geography on the Southern horizon from Knott (*Northern Fells*) even draws an admission from AW that it is 'an untidy mess', although I don't think we can blame him for the way the landscape was formed!

But such lapses are rare. Almost all of the *Guide* is within an inch of perfection. My own list of favourite sections is long but even in abbreviated form would include Pavey Ark 10, Sergeant Man 12, Sour Milk Gill featured in Tarn Crag 10 (all in *The Central Fells*) and Bowfell 10, 13 &14, Wast Water screes, Whin Rigg 9 & 10 (*Southern Fells*). An entirely different

The Lie of the Land... Alan Albion - who set me off on my Wainwright adventure – holding his 1960s Ordnance Survey map (which showed the railway line to Keswick still operational) together with AW's hand drawn maps.

type of summit view is seen in Skiddaw Little Man 4 (*Northern Fells*) and from the final *Western Fells* I'd pick High Stile 1 & 2 (in spite of those pages suffering from the ravages of bad weather in my copy) and pages 4, 5 & 6 from the Pillar chapter.

AW often gives much more detail than would usually be needed when out on the fells, and such information immensely aids our enjoyment both when planning a journey or after we return from it. The precision contained in a Wainwright summit map or shown on an ascent route can make even today's 1:25,000 OS map seem sparse by comparison, and that leads to my fourth reason for claiming his work is exceptional.

Every page of the *Guide* exemplifies a quality that was of fundamental importance to Wainwright – the thoroughness of his research and his unrivalled knowledge of Lakeland as a whole. It is one the key foundations of the *Guide*. Other people know more about individual valleys or mountains, but I have never met anyone who was so versed and knowledgeable about the whole area.

It is usual when working with artists to discover their concern for such detailed research. Photographers, for example, may find only one kind of film suits their needs and are dismayed if they suspect the manufacturer has changed the formula. Darkroom chemicals must be mixed with the upmost precision and their temperature must be kept accurate to within a fraction of one degree. Or a particular lens suits their own vision. When you see a fine art photographer who can produce images of such delicacy they appear almost three-dimensional, it is clear that such research is not simply an end in itself. However, I have never met anyone who was so obsessed with it as AW and it informed the text throughout the seven volumes. It matters to Wainwright that the Ordnance Survey maps of the time were confused as to which watercourse should be named Sobby Gill (Glaramara 6, *Southern Fells*) or that AW had made a rare mistake and written Styhead Tarn as two words not one (Great End 4, *Southern Fells*).

He delighted in the unusual, having discovered that the western slopes of Bowscale Fell feed the River Eden in the east and, vice versa, the eastern watercourses find their way west to the Derwent (Bowscale Fell 2, *Northern Fells)*. He had also studied the Lakeland writers who preceded him and used this knowledge to good effect throughout the *Guide*. He laments that, unlike the Victorians on their Grand Tour of the Lakes, few people now visit Bowscale Tarn, adding, 'the Victorian travellers were right – their sense of values was always sound' (Bowscale Fell 7, *Northern Fells*). He was also happy to acknowledge the work of earlier writers on Lakeland's industrial past such as John Postlethwaite's *Mines and Mining in the Lake District*, first published in 1877 (Carrock Fell 4, *Northern Fells*). Curiosities, oddities and quirks of nature were also favourites, although I think my life would be no less rich for not knowing that the two places with 'cat' in their name – Catbells and Catstycam – can both be seen in a straight line from the summit of Causey Pike (Causey Pike 7, *North Western Fells*). Precision was an integral part of Wainwright's DNA, so it was important to mention that whether Bowfell could be seen from the top of Maiden Moor depends on where you think is the highest point (Maiden Moor 7, *North Western Fells*).

Reading the *Guide* is, for the off-comer, an education into Lakeland culture and history. For example, in the small area around the Langdale Pikes we are informed about the stone axe factories and especially those on Pike o'Stickle (Pike o'Stickle 3, *Central Fells*) and we discover that Stickle Tarn was dammed to provide water for the gunpowder works at Elterwater in the early 19th century (Harrison Stickle 10, *Central Fells*)

Unsurprisingly this research provoked a response from some readers, who were not always convinced that Wainwright was correct. AW was happy to take them on and defend his corner. To those who said that they had identified additional fells to those noted in his summit views, he tartly replied that the diagrams had always been labelled as showing just the principal fells and was keen to explain his methodology (Scoat Fell 9, *Western Fells*).

Wainwright's obsession with such factors was accompanied by a desire to be comprehensive, and that has caused controversy over the years. I don't propose to reopen the arguments about his inclusion of Jack's Rake on Pavey Ark (Pavey Ark 5 & 6, *Central Fells*) or, to a lesser extent, Lord's Rake on Scafell (Scafell 3 & 4, *Southern Fells*), other than to say this. When talking to AW it was clear that he could not have contemplated a work that was not comprehensive and the thought of not including such prominent features was anathema to him.

There's another aspect to Wainwright's work that marks it from all others, and this is the fifth reason for celebrating his *Guide*. As a young man he had produced sketches and cartoons to amuse his office colleagues in Blackburn Town Hall. For a man often portrayed, at least in latter life, as difficult, socially awkward and taciturn, this shows a different side of his complex character. These early works showcase not only his emerging penmanship, but also his sense of humour. It is not the humour of pub jokes, but a mischievous streak that, when the books were first published, had widespread appeal. It permeates all seven volumes, often seeping out of the pages when you least expect it and having the effect of making the reader pay close attention.

The area around Rakefoot farm, just south of Keswick, was not explored, and therefore remained unmapped, 'having regard to the proximity of a bull' (Bleaberry Fell 3, *Central Fells*). A space is reserved for when he makes a successful ascent of the Lion and the Lamb above Grasmere but, sadly, when the book was printed 'such an announcement cannot be made' (Helm Crag 8, *Central Fells*) A shelter alongside the Walna Scar road is 'just big enough for one person or a honeymoon couple' (Dow Crag 4, *Southern Fells*) and while praising a publication by the Forestry Commission on the Roman fort at Hardknott he adds that in terms of its description of walking routes, 'It isn't as good as *The Southern Fells*...not by a long chalk' (Hard Knott 2, *Southern Fells*). In the same book he recounts having tried to ascend Broad Stand on Scafell since the 1930s but that his lack of success is 'amply compensated by the pleasures of going on living' (Scafell 3, *Southern Fells*). One final example also has a measure of self-interest. After drawing a 'Do Not Start Fire' notice next to his map of Harter Fell, AW adds... 'and so waste the effort in drawing all the little trees on this map. The Forestry Commission, too, will be annoyed' (Harter Fell 4, *Southern Fells*).

This quirkiness, which Wainwright developed and expanded as the books progressed, shows not only an increased confidence on his part but also charts the rapport he built up with his readers. And these humorous nuggets make us part of his enterprise and help us identify with it. We feel we know this reclusive author and, in the unlikely event that we would spend time together, we would, from his writing, almost certainly recognise him. We would like to feel that, in our love of the high places of Lakeland, we are kindred spirits, members of a wider community who understand and respect this landscape and want to protect it. In other words, part of a kinship of the fells.

So to my sixth and final reason why I believe AW's *Pictorial Guide to the Lakeland Fells* are important works of literature. It is their *strong authorial voice.* Within the overall structure Wainwright had chosen for the *Guide* he had allowed considerable scope to share his views on Lakeland. I still thought the *Personal Notes in Conclusion* with which each book ends were something of a misnomer. After all, AW has been giving his personal view throughout each volume and his voice comes through loud and clear. Here was an author who does not like what he views as unnecessary change (even in the 1950s and 60s) and who yearns for Lakeland to be like the place he first visited in the 1930s. There are the big issues: for example, the widening of the A66 and the bypassing of Threlkeld with AW arguing that those seeking to destroy the tranquillity of the lakes should be kept out rather than let in. As a non-driver he wanted the roads to be 'no better than is needed for local traffic' (Blencathra 8, *Northern Fells*). But it wasn't just the speedy motorist who comes in for censure. Almost as bad were the walkers who cut off corners and inflicted on beautifully made and well graded paths 'deep stony gashes' (Pike o'Stickle 4, *Central Fells*) and those who destroyed useful cairns and built superfluous ones (Dale Head 9, *North Western Fells*). On that page AW berates the 'lunatics', who are 'loose on the hills' and those walkers are contrasted with the traditional Lakeland craftspeople – contrasted, and found wanting. Old is usually better in AW's eyes and the machines used to build new bridges cannot compare with the craftsmen of a century or more ago (Lank Rigg 3, *Western Fells*) or the quarrymen with their 'ingenious devices and engineering feats...of pre-machine days' (Wetherlam 3, *Southern Fells*).

It is easy to think that Wainwright looked at the Lake District through the rose-tinted glasses of successive generations of off-comers, but his sincerity should not be doubted, nor the passion with which he expressed those views. When he mourns the passing of the traditional builders, that lament comes from the heart: 'The tragedy of our age is that we are not ashamed'.

I have spent the last 30 years exploring the Scottish highlands and islands. Today they are much more frequented than in the 1980s and even more so from Wainwright's initial holiday visits. However, in some places, such as here in the far north, traces of the old narrow single track road are still evident and I can visualise AW walking along with his pipe smouldering; camera at the ready and wondering where he might stay the night.

In a similar vein he bemoans a civilisation where 'men are clever enough to make atomic bombs... yet can't even make a blade of grass or sprig of heather' (Skiddaw Little Man 13, *Northern Fells*). For AW the world as a whole and Lakeland as a specific locality are viewed as places that are becoming more 'discordant and noisy'. One where 'natural sanctuaries are shrinking fast but were never in greater need' (Great Sca Fell 2, *Northern Fells*).

Curiously, his view of the afforestation of great swathes of Lakeland is more contradictory. I find it surprising that he takes a benign view of the Forestry Commission's work on Dodd (Dodd 2-8, *Northern Fells*) and suspect he was influenced by the booklets they had produced. Later, of course, that view was to profoundly change. With good reason he is scathing about Ennerdale (Pillar 3 & 7 and Steeple 4, *Western Fells*) and that scorn also extends to fells like Grike (Grike 2, *Western Fells*). However, he is not opposed to all such planting and makes a case for the Forestry Commission having improved the land around Blengdale (Caw Fell 8, *Western Fells*). Wainwright did not confine his comments to human influence on the fells and had no hesitation in passing judgement on the landscape itself. Pity Great Dodd. A fell that holds 'no appeal to walkers', offers 'no excitement', while all routes of ascent from Dockray 'are uninspiring and dreary' (Great Dodd 2 & 6, *Eastern Fells*).

As each volume of the *Guide* was published and enthusiastically received, we find him using his pages not only to express his own passions and prejudices, but also as a forum for discussion. He explains the problems facing any mapmaker when dealing with rough ground and complicated terrain and the difficulty of having too much information (such as merging contour lines), but not enough space to include them all (Scafell 6, *Southern Fells*). Here too is an author happy to discuss the distinction between achievement and satisfaction when climbing the fells (Ard Crag 3, *North Western Fells*) or to argue that an experienced fellwalker would never trudge along the road where there is a decent bus service (Dale Head 4, *North Western Fells*).

We discover that his appreciation isn't limited to what is obviously attractive but can also be found 'in things desolate and derelict' on the ascent of Swirl How from Coniston. He finds the route through the old copper workings is 'an excellent expedition'. (Swirl How 4, *Southern Fells*). There is also some unorthodox or plain quirky advice, such as suggesting a descent from Kirk Fell may best be achieved in 'bare or stockinged feet' – advice that used to be given to climbers on wet rock but never, so far as I'm aware, to walkers. Certainly I won't be trying it any time soon.... (Kirk Fell 6, *Western Fells*). One difficulty faced by AW is insurmountable: there is no guarantee the *Guide* will be read in chronological order, so information needs to be repeated. This means the bus routes from Keswick to Skiddaw appear in more than one place, yet AW doesn't tell the reader exactly where they go (Skiddaw 9 & 17, *Northern Fells*). Wainwright is also not afraid to point out when other writers are inaccurate. Such authors are castigated for publishing incomplete and misleading details of an ascent of Whin Rigg from Nether Wasdale (Whin Rigg 5, *Southern Fells*)

However, in view of the subsequent breakup of his first marriage, there are times when Wainwright reveals more than he might have originally intended. There are a number of derogatory comments about wives and women in general scattered throughout the *Guide* and these strike a discordant note with the modern reader. Wainwright, as I saw every time we met, was devoted to his second wife Betty and her beneficial influence on him cannot be overestimated, but for the record it is important to look at these comments. They provide, I believe, a valuable insight into AW's mind at the time he was writing the *Guide*. Some of these comments appear gratuitous and perhaps none more so that what I believe is AW's first reference to his marital situation. Towards the end of a lengthy discussion about caves in Lakeland, Wainwright sensibly observes that the abandoned man-made caves can be extremely dangerous and should not be entered. So far so good, until the penultimate sentence, 'Husbands should think of their wives, after which gloomy contemplation, many no doubt will march cheerfully in to a possible doom' (Rosthwaite Fell 3, *Southern Fells*). Later in the same book, AW says he is surprised that these abandoned workings are not 'half-choked' with 'women whose husbands have tired of them' (Wetherlam 8, *Southern Fells*).

Sometimes the tone is lighter, such as when he observes that women climbing over barbed wire must watch their 'bloomers', before adding, 'or whatever they call them nowadays'. A final sentence offers an apology: 'a man whose only passion is for the hills cannot be expected to be well informed in such matters' (Skiddaw 19, *Northern Fells*) and to set this comment in its proper historical context, this book was published in 1962. Even with that caveat, from the first time I annotated the *Guide* in the early 1980s, I felt there was an unremitting bleakness about many of these asides. For example, do the Swan Hotel and the Bishop of Barf really go together, 'even more so than love and marriage' (Barf 2, *North Western Fells*)? And when AW describes the ascent of Robinson from Newlands Hause he cannot resist adding that, given almost the whole route is in view, 'the wife, left in the car, will be watching every move!' (Robinson 6, *North Western Fells*). This might be read as a harmless aside, but Wainwright, with his keen knowledge of Lakeland history, will have been aware that women had been an integral part of the walking and climbing scene for many years.

When the final part of the *Guide*, *The Western Fells*, was published in 1966, AW, in describing the Gable Girdle, informs us that boots (not shoes) are mandatory and that the traverse is suitable for 'well-behaved women – but nagging wives should be left to paddle their feet in Styhead Tarn' (Great Gable 9, *Western Fells*). That, 'well-behaved women' phrase also appears two pages later, and I have always felt that a number of factors had come together at this point in Wainwright's life. His grand undertaking – one unequalled in the history of guidebook writing – was almost at an end. Not only was he contemplating future work, but Wainwright was someone who could not, until the very last months of his life, consider living without a project to which he could devote his attention and energy. He had also found, in Betty McNally, his perfect woman and was writing to her regularly, yet could not, as yet, establish the new life with her that he desperately wanted. At home, events were at breaking point and by September 1966, his first wife Ruth had left. At the beginning of the last book in the *Guide* there is a somewhat backhanded compliment to her, 'for not standing in my way'. Why backhanded? It was clear to me that whatever Ruth may or may not have done, nothing would have prevented Wainwright from completing the task in hand. A final contributing factor was probably his impending retirement, planned for January 1967. For a man who craved order and certainty, all these factors pointed in the opposite direction. As an aside, I never heard AW say anything derogatory about women – either in the privacy of his own home or when working with the film crew.

At his best many of Wainwright's books are outstanding, and any one of them would be achievement enough for many authors. But behind those works is an extremely complex human being, a person whose works inspired widespread praise – even adulation – but who was both confident and insecure in equal measure and who had constructed his own set of defences that almost everyone found impenetrable. The fells gave solace from the 'disappointments and unkindnesses of life' (*Some Personal Notes in Conclusion, Far Eastern Fells*), but that does not mean they obliterated them. Taken as a whole, Wainwright's achievement is without equal. Today literally millions of people see Lakeland through his eyes, and will continue to do so for the foreseeable future.

Trouble at the printers

I was personally very sorry when
Wainwright decided that Michael
Joseph should take over the books
that had previously been printed by the
Westmorland Gazette, although this is
not a reflection on a highly reputable
publishing house. AW believed that an
energetic London publisher would bring
his original books to a wider readership
and hence increase the money received
by his charity. But I was sad nonetheless. I
thought that another part of Wainwright's
heritage was vanishing. I also felt sympathy
for Andrew Nichol, the Gazette's printing
manager, who had kept an ever watchful
eye over them for many years and who
always had their celebrity author's best
interests at heart. When AW told me the
news, I could understand his reasoning,
but said it seemed a pity.

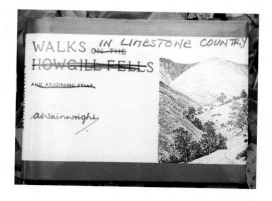

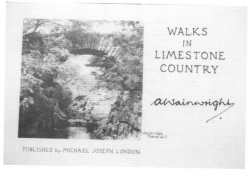

This new arrangement had not long been implemented when I arrived at Kendal Green
to find Wainwright very upset. 'Look at this', he said handing me a copy of what I thought
was *Walks on the Howgill Fells*. When I asked what was wrong, there was a point of the
pipe and an instruction to examine the contents. At first I couldn't see the problem but
then I realised what was exercising AW. Inside, bound in error, was *Walks in Limestone
Country* and, worse still, Michael Joseph had sent this copy to Wainwright to show him
their handiwork. I double checked and *Walks on the Howgill Fells* was on both the dust
jacket and the spine of the book. Equally, walks around Ingleton, an ascent of Whernside
and the caves of Ribblehead made up the contents. For a man whose life was based
around order, this was a disaster.

Wainwright was furious and, taking a black marker pen, made a hasty alteration on the
cover. For once his writing lacked its normal precision and still fuming he added, 'This is
hopeless… here, you can have it if you like'.

The most rare of Wainwright books or just an interesting curiosity?

8. A Scottish
odyssey

A Scottish odyssey. During my research trip to the Isle of Skye there was a week of unrelenting torrential rain. Two weeks later it was almost Mediterranean and gave us one of our best week's filming. This early morning view is from the summit of Sgurr na Stri looking to Soay and Rum in the distance. Many would argue it is the best viewpoint in Britain, although Wainwright favoured an evening view from Elgol.

In the summer and autumn of 1986, AW and I talked about more filming. Our first series had carved out a niche in the BBC2 schedule and, to many people, had become essential viewing. There were two principal reasons for this success. Wainwright was a one-off. The most cursory glance at his work reveals a highly individualistic approach that goes far beyond his handwritten text and detailed illustrations. Look more carefully and the pages reveal not only a general philosophy about life but also pithy comments about an enormous range of topics from his unhappy marriage to the blundering force of big companies, to the place of the individual within society. The television films added a new dimension to this. What appealed to many viewers was more than simply the retiring figure who shunned the limelight. Wainwright would often say least when the landscape was at its most majestic. When most presenters would feel the urge to explain what we can clearly see for ourselves, Wainwright said little or nothing.

There was a second reason for the films' success. There are untold numbers of people who love Britain's wild places and our remote, windswept summits, quiet valleys and glens. These are people who can look at the sweep of a landscape or a bowl of hills tumbling down to a lake side and be reduced to tears. This is a community of like-minded souls that used to be underserved by television. Yet in 1985, labouring for many months in the editing room over the first series, I had little idea how much impact the films would create. Fortunately, there were no focus groups to make comments on trial programmes; no string of middle management to please and no overnight ratings to worry about. The films were made, quite simply, because I wanted to make them.

Wainwright had often talked about his Scottish expeditions and, when I heard about how he had made these trips from the 1930s onwards always using public transport, expedition was clearly the right word. Unlike our first series, where every programme was based on one of his guidebooks, our Scottish films had only his set of *Scottish Mountain Drawings* as a basis, with little text to help me. I also had other reservations. AW was now approaching 80, his general health was getting worse and the distances both to and within Scotland are far greater. Unlike the first series, where he and Betty often returned home in the evening, we would need to allow time for travel and find appropriate hotels. 'But nothing too expensive, Richard', warned our reluctant star, 'and no fancy food'.

In a series of five journeys we revisited parts of Scotland that had most impressed AW. They were places he had given up hope of ever revisiting and that made our filming all the more poignant. We travelled to the rugged, rock-scoured landscape of Sutherland where the ancient gneiss breaks through in a succession of prominent peaks that, although not objectively high, tower over a landscape often dotted with innumerable small lochans and, occasionally, larger expanses of water. The coastline is never far away and it is that mixture of sea and mountain, together with its remote location – some 650 miles and more from London – that give this area its special character. There are places here that have not significantly changed in the last half-century. Later we made an emotional return to Skye with the island bathed in glorious days of long sun and few clouds. Included in our itinerary was Glen Coe – where, not surprisingly, the weather was less kind – and our Scottish trip finished with three fine, but very different mountain ranges – those of Torridon, Kintail and the Cairngorms.

AW's original journeys north of the border began with his visit to Arran in 1936 while still working in his native Blackburn. They were major undertakings, especially given the time available. They started by train but later Wainwright made use of MacBraynes' buses to reach as many corners as possible of the sparsely populated country north of the Central Belt. This company has been synonymous with travel in the Scottish highlands for over a century, providing passenger and freight services from the mainland to many islands. Their bus service, which AW came to rely on, began in 1906 and soon expanded. Their distinctive red, cream and green livery was a common sight across the highlands and islands until the early 1970s.

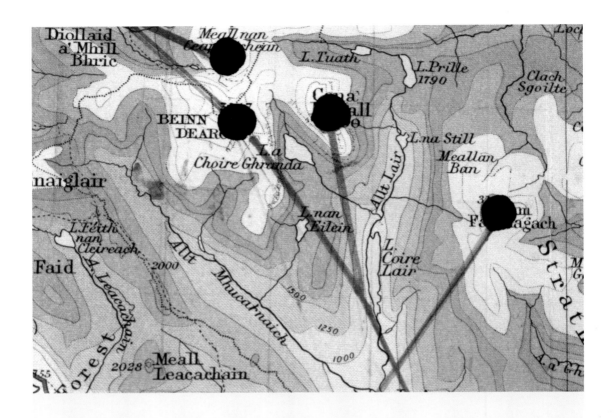

One day AW asked if I would like to see how he had planned his six volume Scottish Mountain Drawings. As he opened his Bartholomew ½ inch maps of Scotland I was amazed that his planning was almost as detailed as his original Guide. Each summit had been given a red circle and a line drawn indicating his preferred viewpoint. Once a usable photograph had been obtained, the circle was inked in black. Many of these viewpoints were relatively low, but still involved a long walk in.

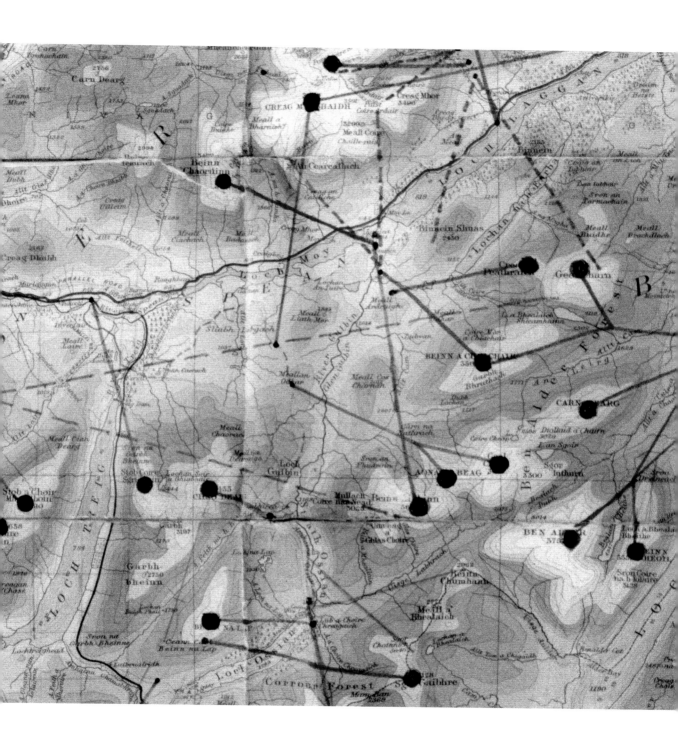

The journeys we undertook would be very different. Betty would drive Wainwright north, often stopping overnight. En route were regular pauses at cafes and tea shops – many of which AW remembered from his original trips. We began in the autumn of 1986, but without any of the production team. AW and Betty often rented the same holiday home – a wooden chalet at Duirinish, south of Plockton on the west coast – and, much to my surprise, I had been invited along. I had cycled around much of the west coast and some of the islands 12 years earlier and had been a regular visitor to Scotland since then. But Wainwright wanted me to see this landscape through his eyes. In effect, to show off his favourite places and ensure we captured them on camera.

I thought we made an odd sight, AW tall and top heavy, the slightly built, petite Betty and me, some 40 and more years younger. We covered many miles that week, Wainwright providing a running commentary in a way that belied his taciturn public persona. AW had planned each day with his usual meticulous attention to detail: a trip to Skye included a visit to Elgol, so I could see that often photographed panorama of the Cuillin. He was convinced it was the finest view of that jagged mountain range. Later in the day we saw these hills from the west having driven down to Glen Brittle and the campsite there. On another day we looked at the Five Sisters of Kintail from a variety of locations and Betty nudged her little car precariously over the Mam Ratagan pass and down to Glenelg. We even ventured as far as Torridon where AW had a special affection for Lochs Clair and Coulin and the view they gave of those giants Beinn Eighe and Liathach.

At the start of planning these Scottish programmes, AW produced a set of half-inch Bartholomew maps that had formed the basis for his original journeys. What surprised me were not the maps themselves, but what he had drawn on them. Unlike the 1:25,000 maps of the Pennine Way (where his annotations covered large areas of the map), neatly drawn on each map in red ink were a series of lines that showed where the best views were to be obtained. These, in turn, had formed the basis for his drawings. In earlier years limited time had prevented Wainwright from making ascents of all the mountains over 3,000 feet – the Munros – and he decided his holidays would be better spent trying to see as many of them as possible, rather than climbing just a few. Later on, advancing years and commitments to other work again meant that becoming a Munroist – or 'completer' in the jargon of Munro-bagging – would be impossible. He settled instead for drawing all of them, along with some peaks of lesser height and a number of prominent landmarks. The result is his *Scottish Mountain Drawings* which were published between 1974 and 1979, so Scotland was still very much in his mind as we embarked on our filming.

Scotland is on an altogether different scale to the Lake District, not just in terms of the mountains and their height but, equally importantly, in their isolation and the long walks in that are often necessary. It was almost 400 miles to Kinlochbervie for our first programme on the far north and the journey was spread over two days.

But it was not simply the logistics that were different from our first series. AW himself had changed. The man who once had firm views about how he should appear on television, now appeared to embrace the process and was enjoying his time with the film crew. He was usually patient when we needed to do retakes or had to wait for the rain to ease. Betty told me how being with younger people, revisiting favourite places and the success of the programmes had all had a positive effect. There was, though, something special about returning north of the border. It was, he said, 'a very sentimental journey'. We recreated part of that by setting off on the train from Oxenholme station with AW sitting opposite Eric in a first-class carriage. After checking I had got a third off the fare by showing his Senior Railcard, AW needed little prompting: it was, he said, 'a reminder of the years after the war when, for about thirty years, I used to come regularly in May and September, getting on the train at Oxenholme and heading north'. Wainwright talked about 'showing off Scotland' to Eric, although he added, 'we haven't time to do everything I'd like to see. But I'll try and pick out the highlights, the places I like best'. In Scotland the landscape is drawn on a larger canvas. The Lake District has just four mountains over 3,000 feet, Scotland not far short of 300. Eric Robson has quite rightly remarked that Wainwright could not 'tame' Scotland in the way he had the Lake District.

Until the recent introduction of the North Coast 500 – Scotland's answer to America's Route 66, which includes the A838 to Durness – you could travel on these supposed A-roads and meet few other travellers. In 1987, you might drive for an hour of more before passing another car. Only in July and August were visitors noticeable and, even then, their numbers were comparatively small. Wainwright had been extremely resourceful in making maximum advantage of the train and bus timetables in his visits north of the border, but even so there were a few places that had eluded his best efforts. One of these was Cape Wrath.

Getting to this most north-westerly point on the British mainland is not for the faint-hearted – it is a chancy business. In the short summer season a passenger ferry runs from the crofting community of Keoldale, two miles south-west of Durness. The brief journey across the Kyle of Durness is tide and weather dependent and there is an awkward scramble into and out of the small boat at either end.

All but the most hardy or hard-up then board what, in 1987, was a rattling minibus. This slowly follows the undulating rough track for the final 16 miles to the headland. Our journey was even more difficult. Filming in advance of the tourist season, we had to make special arrangements for the ferryman to take us across. Then I hit what seemed an immovable obstacle; the minibus would not be on the headland but away having its annual service and MOT. To my immense frustration, it would not be back until a few weeks after our filming. Additionally, getting it back to the headland was an intricate operation necessitating two landing craft being fixed together and the bus placed astride them.

After many phone calls (together with the offer of some financial help from the BBC and a starring role in the film), the owners managed to get everything completed ahead of schedule and the bus ready and in place for our filming. AW was impressed by everyone's efforts and thrilled, at last, to be making this journey. When we finally disembarked at Cape Wrath, he was eloquent about the Atlantic waging a war against the headland from the time it was formed. So far so good. Then Eric asked if, having taken 80 years to get here, it was worth the effort. We all listened expectantly for an answer that would sum up AW's long held desire to reach this isolated point of the British mainland and his joy at having finally made it. 'I'm glad I've seen it', was the sparse reply. Eric, nonplussed by the brevity and out of earshot of Betty, muttered something about not holding AW back if he went near the cliff edge in future. Later I asked AW about the day and we got a few more sentences to add to this scene, but it showed me yet again that he was a person who always preferred to let the landscape do the talking.

When Wainwright first travelled through these remote corners of Scotland, a missed bus connection could mean a wait of 24 hours or more. That all changed when Betty appeared. Making no mention of his first marriage, Wainwright spoke of 'acquiring' a wife who brought her car 'as a dowry'. When he visited in the 1940s and 50s accommodation was scarce and the journey north was made extremely slow by the so-called main road – the A838 – being single-track with passing places. There were also a number of ferry crossings, such as the one at Kylesku where the sea pushes far inland into the twin lochs of Glendhu and Glencoul and forms a formidable natural barrier. Wainwright considered this 'the most romantic place along the west coast of Scotland' and while the modern road bridge saves hours, he thought there was 'no magic about it. There was magic about the ferry boat. I've spent hours here waiting for the ferry and not regretting a moment of it. The scenery is so superb around here. We're looking at a scene here that hasn't changed for thousands of years'. Wainwright was taking us back to a time that had long vanished and to walks that were more expeditionary than those he undertook in Lakeland.

We started our Scottish odyssey in the far north. The bridge at Kylesku had opened only 3 years previously and as AW & Eric sat near the now disused slipway at Kylestrome on the northern shore of Loch Glendhu, Wainwright expressed his regret that the ferry had been replaced by the new road. He told me that time spent here waiting for the boat on a summer's evening was never wasted.

Looking out across the vast expanse of the Atlantic at Cape Wrath. After all the trouble taken by the local community to get AW here for his much anticipated first visit, we had hoped he would be keen to enthuse about this most north-western point of mainland Britain. This was one of many occasions when Wainwright preferred the landscape to do the talking.

His longest day was over 26 miles from Ullapool to Lochinver, through a landscape that is little inhabited and where he met neither a car or another person.

Sutherland is the least populated part of the British mainland but the scale of this area – let alone the scale of the whole country – meant that Wainwright was a guest. He was a fascinated and inquisitive visitor, but in spite of his annual visits, he was not an expert. One particular frustration was the Gaelic names. 'I've climbed many of the mountains in Scotland', AW told me, 'and never been able to tell anybody because I couldn't pronounce the names'. This gave me an excuse to introduce a guest into each programme. I thought Wainwright might object to this plan, seeing an additional person as either an intrusion or an attempt to steal the limelight. Surprisingly, the opposite occurred. Once he realised that a carefully chosen guest could add to his knowledge and enjoyment of an area, the idea was welcomed.

The Joy of Filming

We received many offers of help during our filming — and one or two bizarre refusals. Planning to film near Strathcarron I contacted a landowner who had recently purchased an estate and moved up from London. After agreeing we could be on his land, he asked if I could do him a favour. "What's that?' I asked. 'Well... its a bit complicated but there's a woman locally I've got to know and really like. Would it be possible to bring her along to see the filming?'. Having said that would not be a problem but filming could sometimes be boring to watch, I agreed. He had a further request, 'If it's possible to treat me, um, like an assistant director that would be helpful'. Anything, I thought, for the course of true love.

Another incident particularly amused AW. I had spoken to the owner of many thousands of acres in the north-west highlands. Again I was asking permission to film on part of his vast estate and explained exactly what was required. 'But that's not mine', he replied and told me to ring his neighbour. On making this second call I was surprised to learn that the land did, after all, belong to the person I had previously called. Feeling a bit like a shuttlecock hit from one player to another, I redialled the original number and explained that I had some good news: 'this land is yours after all'. 'Wonderful' came the reply, 'Marvellous. Another few acres, eh?'

Finally, AW had wanted to visit a place that was especially important to him on the west coast, so I duly rang the landowner. He was not easy to track down but eventually I got hold of him and explained what we would like to do. There was a short pause then, in a very public school we-know-best-voice, he replied, 'I'm not having you here. You're all bloody commies. You can't come here'. 'Excuse me', I said, 'I am happy to inform you that our guest's politics are very much to the right of the political spectrum'. But to no avail. 'I don't care, you're all bloody pinkos'. And with that the line went dead.

Camera person Richard Ranken utilising an excellent vantage point to capture a vast seascape. 'Make sure you don't fall',
was AW's advice, followed by, 'what are you looking at?' 'Sea', came Richard's reply, 'and more sea'.

The late Finlay MacRae was a forester by profession with expert knowledge of the remote Glen Dessarry, west of Loch Arkaig – knowledge that he generously shared with AW & Eric. Sadly we didn't have time to talk about his other great love – playing the pipes. He was an expert, deeply rooted in its traditions and proud of his Gaelic heritage.

In Sutherland, a retired GP, Dr Pennie, said there was no easy clue to pronouncing the Gaelic names and it was best to ask the locals. Wainwright not only learnt how to pronounce Quinag after years of making the common mistake of thinking the Q sounds the same as in English, but also discovered at first hand what it is like to live in this infertile landscape, one where much of it is unchanged since the last ice age. For a man who was supposed not to like company, AW was enthusiastic throughout the conversation, even when Dr Pennie said he wouldn't like a full set of guidebooks produced for this area – no matter how well illustrated they might be.

What was fascinating during our summer together in Scotland was Wainwright's photographic recall of journeys made 30 or 40 years earlier such as his first ascent of Suilven. This was one of his favourite Scottish hills and he walked the ten miles from the fishing village of Lochinver up the estate track past Glencanisp Lodge to the base of the mountain, before scrambling up Bealach Mor, onto the north-western ridge and finally arriving at the summit. Time had not diminished his memory of that day, when the top had been under ominous black cloud on the walk in, before finally clearing to reveal the stunning views. 'The sort of day you never forget. A wonderful experience'.

But much had changed: AW remembered the village of Shieldaig when the only road came from Lochcarron and then ground to a halt. There were no guesthouses and even the inn had closed. Four decades later Wainwright recalled meeting Mrs Lewis, a widow, who found a bed for him. This detailed recollection of earlier events went far beyond what most of us could manage and, on checking some of AW's information, time and again I found it to be totally accurate. He remembered his first view of the Black Cuillin was from the old bridge near the Sligachan Hotel. On that day the summits of Am Basteir, Sgurr nan Gillean and the like were 'starkly clear'. These mountains were beyond the reach of public transport and a man confined to one week's holiday. It was not until 1954 that AW persuaded a colleague to act as chauffeur. I asked AW to tell Eric a story he had earlier mentioned earlier about the importance of that first visit to Skye: 'I was so anxious to come here that from about 1947 onwards whenever I got a new diary, every year I opened it at random and wrote a note in it: "Have you been to Skye yet?" And of course I came across this during the course of the year but I never came until 1954.'

Like many people, Wainwright's first summit attempt was on Sgurr nan Gillean, the sharp peak that dominates the north-eastern skyline and, like many visitors, he discovered that these mountains are a different proposition from those in Lakeland. Persuading his driving companion to join him, the pair set off for the top, but success eluded them, 'The first day we got within 30 yards of the top and it was getting decidedly airy because it's like climbing a spire and the top of it is almost like a needle. We shirked it about 30 yards from the top and I kicked myself all the way back. We should have gone on. There was no great difficulty. We were just getting precipices on each side. So I persuaded him to come again the next day and we did it and it's a wonderful place to be.' Wainwright didn't like exposed situations and was not a fan of scrambling where both hands and feet are required. When we finished filming at the Sligachan bridge, he called me over and said he had an unusual request. 'Would you and the film crew climb the mountain for me?' The next day, burdened down by the heavy, unwieldy equipment and with the odd curse or two, we set off for the summit. We were helped by local guide Gerry Akroyd, who, like Wainwright, is from Lancashire but has made these hills his home. Sgurr nan Gillean is an ascent that requires a certain amount of nerve but, most importantly, stamina. It was a long, hot day, and without enough water our progress was slow. We were all extremely tired, but somehow we made the summit. The crew's achievement was rewarded by superb views, AW's thanks and the pint he bought us all in the hotel bar. Later, when I showed him the results, he was impressed by the images we had captured on film and, although he struggled to make out the details, felt we had relived his own ascent 30 years earlier. 'It's important', he commented, 'that you get up there and see it for yourself'. That was true but it would have been more helpful if today's lightweight, high-quality cameras had been around in 1987. Fortunately our camera person on this and subsequent series was Richard Ranken. He was fit, a keen rugby player and having been to Sedbergh School with its famous cross-country run (arguably the toughest in Britain), knew more than the rest of us about suffering.

The Skye film also contains the most extraordinary scene we ever filmed with Eric and AW. At the end of Glen Brittle the road stops at the campsite. The beach lies ahead and the Cuillin dominate the view east. Wainwright was annoyed because earlier I stopped to film some shots of the Cuillin ridge that I knew we would need. I had been here two weeks earlier on a recce and, after checking a number of possible locations, had made my choice. It was late afternoon, so with an eye on the time, I had managed to get everyone out of our various cars as quickly as possible. The tripod had been set up, camera mounted and light readings taken, when AW approached me and said, 'Richard, this isn't the best place – you passed that earlier'. My protests went unheeded and what had started as a mild disagreement was escalating into a full-blown argument. Eventually Betty called a truce, reminding me that 'Red is usually right'. So we all got back into our vehicles, performed u-turns and retraced our steps. Unfortunately it was the rarest of occasions when AW wasn't correct and at Betty's insistence a grudging apology was offered. I tried to explain that a film camera saw the landscape differently from one that took stills, but to no avail. Farce almost turned into tragedy when, back at the original location, I was hastily, and in a bad temper, manoeuvring the Land Rover when I caught sight of something moving straight towards the front bumper and rapidly applied the brakes, an inch or two short of AW's lumbering frame. Injuring your star was not, I admitted to myself, probably the best career move.

The aftermath of our disagreement was still simmering when we got to our final location at head of the glen. Nearby is an area of grass which Wainwright and Eric walked onto. At AW's insistence, the pair sat back to back. 'That'll teach him. He won't be able to film this.' AW was talking about me to Eric not realising that, with the radio microphones switched on, I could hear every word. I was setting off to intervene when Richard Ranken called me back. 'Just let them do it', he suggested, 'It will be fantastic'. And he was right. It looked great but there was also another unforeseen benefit.

Without this photograph many people might doubt that AW really did sit back to back with Eric Robson at Glen Brittle. Eric has a look of wry amusement, Wainwright is distinctly irritable. Nevertheless, this was one of the most memorable scenes we captured on film.

Wainwright, realising that far from calling him and Eric to order, we were quite content to film, took control of the situation by talking eloquently and knowledgeably about Sgurr Dearg and the other peaks that make up the southern part of the ridge.

That summer also saw Wainwright grounded in the wind and rain of Glen Coe; battling the midges in Glen Nevis; and disappointed that the views weren't better in the Mamores, but these were minor inconveniences set against the pleasure of being in Scotland again. With the exception of our spat on Skye, this was a man who was not only delighted to share his memories and insights but who was pleased to meet strangers, be it the former distinguished forester, Finlay MacRae, talking about the uncertificated teacher who once taught in the tiny hut of a school in Glen Dessarry or the author and climber, Ken Crocket, explaining that the Victorian observatory that once stood on the summit of Ben Nevis was for meteorological not astronomical purposes. Our summer together was characterised by smiles rather than scowls, even when admitting that long legs prevented AW from climbing. 'It's not that I don't like heights, but I'm too clumsy on rocks. Legs are far too long... they get in the way, instead of being a help'.

Wainwright in Scotland had been 18 months in the making and now the end, at least as far as the filming was concerned, was in sight. It was a series of journeys that finished with the first snows of winter already lying on the summits. Wainwright and Betty had mixed feelings about this particular project. The journeys to and from Kendal had taken time and demanded a lot of energy from both of them and the filming itself would have been tiring for a person half AW's age. Balanced against this was the sheer joy of seeing places that AW had thought were confined to his memory; of discovering how little of Scotland had changed since he first made his way across these landscapes with train and bus timetables metaphorically in one hand and his trusty Ensign camera in the other.

It was early autumn when we set off to make our final film, traversing the magnificent and defiant mountains that make up the Cairngorms. While they lack the obvious drama and grandeur of other places, they more than make up for that with their height, bulk, wild isolation and subtlety. Braeriach, Loch Einich (now called Eanaich on OS maps), Cairn Toul, Ben Macdui, the Lairig Ghru, Glen Derry and, of course, Cairngorm itself, are elemental places that once visited are imprinted on the memory. These are places that repay serious exploration and an understanding that each summit has its own special characteristics and atmosphere. To group them together simply as 'the Cairngorms', as on most maps, is to miss the point. Within these glens and summits are places that can be as wild as anywhere in Europe – not only in winter but on any day of the year. To try to capture on film this area of desolate beauty and sub-Arctic wilderness, we would start our journey in the west and finish in the east. Wainwright had first come here by train, alighting at Aviemore. Once a picturesque village of predominantly wooden cottages either side of the main street, it suffered from a poorly designed central development that, even in 1987, had seen better days. This was a community transformed beyond recognition from the days when visitors arrived with tweed coats and heavy rucksacks. Although our time for filming was short, AW still wanted to see the havoc caused by insensitive planning. Failing eyesight was no barrier to his view on the new Aviemore Centre. He pronounced this 'a mess' and few would disagree with him. Today it has been redeveloped yet again but many feel it is still a mixed blessing.

Wainwright's happiness was restored as we left the bustle and trippers behind. Soon he was once again by the shores of Loch an Eilein in Rothiemurchus Forest, with its 13th century ruined island castle. This must be one of the most photographed places in Scotland, yet in fair weather or foul, it never fails to impress as you walk underneath the towering Caledonian pines. I was intrigued by how much of this landscape AW had managed to explore in the years before Betty became a willing driver. Wainwright had begun his journeys with the places that were easiest to reach, such as the Ryvoan Pass with its landmark bothy. Later he ventured further afield into the Lairig Ghru, surrounded by the Cairngorm giants. In spite of their proximity, Wainwright told me that he had only managed to climb about 20 Munros in the same number of years. He was already retired when he published his *Scottish Mountain Drawings* and with advancing years, even getting good vantage points for each summit was a significant challenge, involving a walk of up to 12 miles to get to the right place.

A day with the Reindeer

I did make one fleeting appearance in *Wainwright in Scotland*. I appeared in front of the camera during our filming with Alan Smith and the reindeer herd that graze on the slopes just west of the road that goes ever upwards to the Cairngorm ski centre. Fortunately I can't easily be seen. Our filming with Eric, AW and Alan became progressively more chaotic as the herd found us a welcome diversion from their daily routine. Antlers were thrust into the camera lens and it took all of Eric's strength to prevent them barging him out of the shot. These gentle beasts are nonetheless hefty creatures and it is not easy to stand your ground and have a sensible conversation with the camera turning. Eric just about managed to pull it off. Wainwright was less lucky. It was clear to me that the struggle between him and an inquisitive male called Wally was an unequal one.

Wally had been reared by hand and was more docile and demanding than the rest of the herd. Not wanting to stop a conversation that was flowing freely and knowing that the good light was a brief intermission between periods of rain, I was aware that something had to be done before AW was toppled and tumbled off down the hillside. So I stepped in behind AW and hiding behind his broad frame and jacket, kept him upright while the filming continued. Wally was not to be thwarted and the final ten minutes of filming was a battle of wills: Wally wanting all the attention and me holding our star firmly in place. Once the camera had stopped running we could regroup.

Wainwright's comment? 'That was interesting, Richard. I think Wally liked me.'

It is inevitable, I think, that Wainwright's crowning achievement will always be his *Guide*, but that should not prevent us appreciating his *Scottish Mountain Drawings*. While his draughtsmanship may not be as detailed (not helped, I would argue, by the books being a larger format), they are important in understanding the forces that shaped him as an artist and as a person. Imagine, just for a moment, the start of such a project. AW had a thousand photographs. This is an extraordinary collection when film, processing and printing were costly items. Also think about the set of Bartholomew half-inch maps that he bought and then laboriously draw an open circle on each summit that attained the magical Munro height of 3,000 feet. Over the years, once he had seen and photographed each mountain, the circle was then filled in and became a black circle. A smaller black dot and red line showed the direction and location from which the photograph had been taken. Over a period of years all the open circles had been blacked in. While the resultant *Scottish Mountain Drawings* were very different from his original Lakeland *Guide*, the methodology was similar. There was a need for order, for detailed planning, for completion. Many authors, I would suggest, would be content to put their energy into concentrating on fewer mountains and studying them in more detail.

The use of my Land Rover and the help of numerous landowners meant we could journey far into the Cairngorms and this was an unexpected bonus for Wainwright. Braced against the wind and rain he was able to stand once again on the upland shores of Loch Einich with Braeriach dominating the skyline eastwards. 'One of the wildest places in Scotland', was AW's judgement on this landscape. Another bonus was my ability to arrange for AW to meet people he had long admired and top of that list was a man who knows more about the Cairngorms than anyone else. The scientist and ecologist Dr Adam Watson is the author of many important works including, for many years, the Scottish Mountaineering Club's guide to this area which has inspired successive generations of walkers and climbers. Like Wainwright, he is not someone to suffer fools easily and I was apprehensive about how the pair would get on. But my worries were unfounded. I knew AW was looking forward to this meeting but on the day I was taken aback by how thrilled he was. Likewise Adam Watson shared his unrivalled knowledge generously. He was a perfect companion, explaining the attraction of a landscape he has spent his whole life studying and making it accessible to an audience who lacked that understanding.

Manoeuvring AW in and out of boats always concerned me and perhaps because I didn't want to hear the answer, I never asked our star if he could swim. Wainwright always seemed oblivious to any problems and he enjoyed every minute of the crossing from Elgol to Loch Coruisk.

So our summer together ended on a genuine high. Wainwright was delighted by the places we had visited and the mountains, lochs, glens and seascapes we had seen together. As we turned south for the final time there was one surprising admission that I remembered AW making earlier that summer. It came when we were filming high in the Coulin Forest above Achnashellach, when Wainwright said of Scotland, 'I thought it was wonderful. There is nothing like this in the Lake District. It's far wilder, far grander than the Lake District but it hasn't the romantic beauty of the Lake District which appealed to me first of all. I couldn't live here. I'm fond of solitude and loneliness but you get rather too much of it. I still like to go and watch Blackburn Rovers twice a year...'

So much for the popular image of the solitary man. His final words, 'This has been a very special bonus to me', were unsolicited and heartfelt. It had been a wonderful summer.

Meeting the Media

'We'll go first class then... and don't forget my railcard.'

Wainwright's first visit to London was by royal invitation to collect his MBE and I always assumed he would not want to return there. I was amazed, therefore, when he agreed with my suggestion that we should launch our Scottish series in the capital. However, there were strict conditions attached. We had to leave and return on the same day; we were to spend the minimum time possible in London – just enough, in fact, to show one of the films, display the accompanying book and, if absolutely necessary, answer no more than one or two questions. There would be no separate interviews with any of the assembled media and no posing for photographs.

The journey from Oxenholme station went smoothly enough and AW happily settled into his seat in the smoking section. The press conference, hosted by BBC Books, was packed with journalists who were clearly aware that Wainwright's visit was a significant, and unlikely, event. Our star was on his best behaviour but immediately the formalities were concluded he turned to me and whispered, 'I think we should go now'. It was less of a suggestion and more of a command. It was a short taxi ride to Euston station but I was slightly alarmed when I realised the drop-off point was beneath the station concourse. As soon as AW stepped onto the escalator for the short ride upward I realised we were in trouble. AW got on first and I was just below him. Within seconds I became aware of my blunder. Towering above me Wainwright was starting to sway from side to side like a man at sea. 'Are you used to these?' I asked, trying to camouflage my concern. 'No...noooo...' was the reply, at which point AW toppled backwards with me trying to support him. It was an unequal task and Britain's best-known guidebook writer ignominiously arrived feet first and horizontal on the concourse. It took a significant effort to return AW to a vertical position and gave him another reason to dislike big cities.

We had eaten little all day but this early evening train had a restaurant car, so I suggested that we took advantage of it at the BBC's expense. 'I don't think so Richard. We'll have fish and chips in Kendal.' And that's exactly what we did... just before closing time at eleven o'clock, with chips that had been fried much earlier in the night, limp fish and rain streaking down the windows of the car. Illuminated by the Kendal street lights, I could see AW smiling for the first time that day.

Our second, and final, 'meet the media' outing was far more successful. It was late winter with plentiful snow on the summits, as AW and I made our way up the side of Loch Lomond, on past Crianlarich and Tyndrum before, as had been requested by my front seat passenger, catching the last of the light on Rannoch Moor. Earlier in the day Betty had said goodbye to us both on what she called our 'boys weekend away'. We were travelling to the Kings House Hotel, at the entrance to Glen Coe.

The Kings House is steeped in history and, dating from the 17th century, is one of the oldest licensed hostelries in Scotland. Our visit here was another part of the publicity for *Wainwright in Scotland*. In spite of a location far removed from where film launches are normally held, there was no shortage of journalists willing to make the trip, most probably thinking it was an effective way of combining (a little) work with (a lot of) pleasure. In the comfort of the residents' lounge, AW was happy to meet our guests and, given they all had a commitment to the outdoors, to share stories with them.

Unlike our trip to London, Wainwright was in no hurry to get back home. He was happy to be driven around for hours, especially as the elevated seat offered a good view of the hills. During that weekend we visited Glen Etive, slowly journeyed down Glen Coe, went round to Kinlochleven and west towards Oban with a final excursion to Fort William and Glen Nevis. I wanted to check that it was not too exhausting. 'No, no', was the answer, 'I'm enjoying every minute. It's good to be in the hills again, especially in winter when they are forbidding and sombre. Buachaille Etive Mor always looks impressive. Bidean is a favourite and the Aonach Eagach is intimidating...it's not a place for me. No, this has been a wonderful weekend.' And a little while later, 'The press seemed friendly enough too'.

When we got home Betty asked what we had eaten. 'I hope it's not just fish and chips'. Wainwright and I looked at each other. With a clear conscience I said, 'absolutely not'. We had, after all, enjoyed copious quantities of bacon, sausage, eggs, fried bread and a varied assortment of cakes and sticky buns.

In the comfortable isolation of the Kings House at the eastern end of Glen Coe and the junction of Glen Etive, Wainwright was surprisingly keen to meet outdoor writers and journalists who had made the journey here to launch our Scottish films.

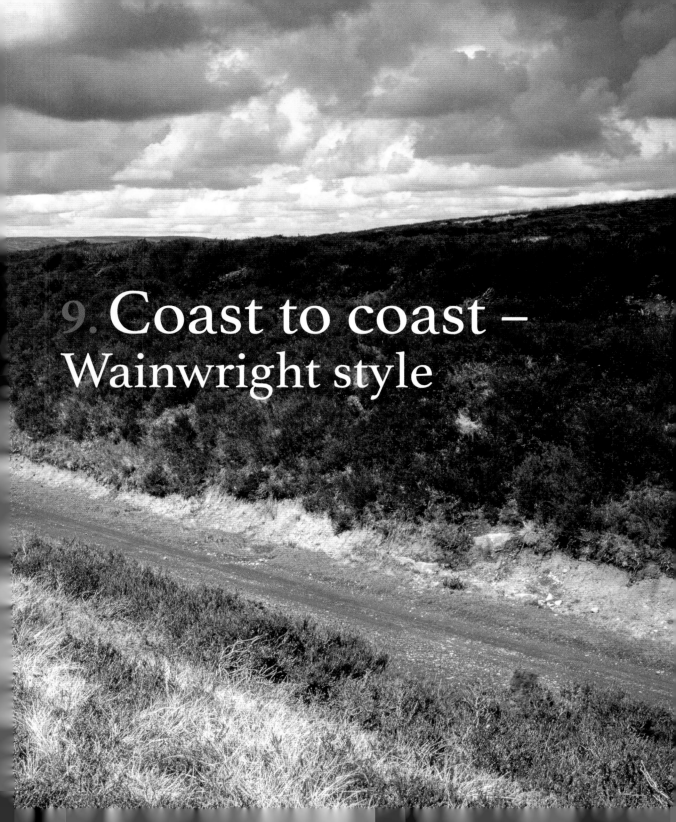

9. Coast to coast –
Wainwright style

Coast to Coast – Wainwright style. Wainwright's Coast to Coast walk follows the line of the old Rosedale railway as it crosses High Blakey Moor. In poor weather this is remote country and without the old trackbed to follow it is easy to get lost. What the landscape lacks in dramatic scenery, it more than compensates for with vast panoramic skies. I watched many CtoCers heading east checking AW's book to see exactly how many miles were still left!

By 1989 Wainwright needed no persuasion to embark on another summer of filming. This biennial process of filming had become part of his routine and the filming and the associated publicity, newspaper reviews and ever-increasing postbag of admiring letters were accepted as part of the package. Even so, AW complained to me that it was now impossible to go anywhere without being recognised. Once seen on television his distinctive profile was known to millions.

We had also found a way of working that suited Betty and AW; one that fitted into their lifestyle and commitments and also ensured that he did not become too exhausted. I thought it a weakness that our first series had, with the exception of that memorable day on Haystacks, something of a random quality about it. I liked my filming to have an overarching theme that bound the individual episodes together, and *Wainwright in Scotland* fulfilled that perfectly. So when I made my regular journeys to 38 Kendal Green in the spring of 1988 it was to let them see how the Scottish films formed a whole. We sat round a newly bought, large and expensive television, the curtains were drawn and the viewing began. Betty would examine AW's performance and consider the film as a whole, 'Red, I think you could have smiled a bit more there...'; 'Eric is good isn't he?' and 'The camera work is excellent'.

Wainwright was peering intently, trying to see how we captured the mountains and glens that had been his friends for over half a lifetime. He was oblivious to his own role or how a difficult scene may have been edited to best effect. For him the landscape was all. 'I think you've done a pretty good job', was his usual comment. Later the conversation would turn to the specifics of the area.

A rare photograph of the CtoC team in Swaledale – minus Betty who was using my camera. From l to r: Lucy Jolly, Production Assistant; Mark Murray, researcher; Mike Riley, sound recordist; yours truly, exact job unknown; Kevin Robertson, assistant camera; Richard Ranken, camera; Eric Robson & AW.

Then we would talk about other mountains we could have filmed; where we might have visited if we had more time or when AW was younger and, always, a comparison of our visit with those he had made years earlier.

As the spring progressed I arrived regularly with a folder of feature articles, favourable reviews and a pile of letters, usually sent to 'A.Wainwright, c/o BBC 2, London'. By the summer we agreed to do another series and now AW needed no persuasion – either about taking part or what it should be. The unanimous choice of AW, Betty and myself – agreed over gooseberry pancakes and before the coffee came – was his *Coast to Coast Walk*. Of more concern to Betty and myself was how we would manage the logistics. We were planning to film from spring to autumn of the following year, 1989, by which time AW would be 82. I had noticed further deterioration in his health. The years of heavy smoking were now having a considerable effect on his breathing and his walking. In spite of Betty's best efforts, AW was still overweight and, being top heavy, extra care was needed on any ground that was uneven or rocky. Yet his mind was still as sharp as ever and the new series was another challenge to be accomplished.

By the time we came to film the CtoC, having a guest was an accepted part of each programme and AW was keen to utilise their specialist knowledge. Tom Clare was the county archaeologist of Cumbria and added enormously to our exploration of the ancient settlement of Severals near Ravenstonedale and the landscape and artefacts nearby.

I have always thought the 190 miles of his route from St. Bees Head in Cumbria to Robin Hood's Bay in North Yorkshire a tremendous feat of planning – a visionary line that, apart from a small section in the Vale of York, is interesting every step of the way. Fortunately, it was easy to see how this might be broken down into four television programmes. The first part would cross Lakeland from the west coast, starting at St Bees Head and taking us through fantastic scenery to Haweswater. In contrast the second film, from Shap Abbey to Keld, featured a landscape less visited and in many ways more remote. The third programme had a strong historical theme, as we set off from the former lead mining village of Gunnerside, wound our way down through the small communities of Swaledale, through the market town of Richmond, before halting at Danby Wiske. Finally we journeyed from the wonderfully preserved ruins of Mount Grace Priory, across the bleak and sometimes featureless terrain of the North York Moors to journey's end at Robin Hood's Bay. 'You can get excellent fish and chips there Richard.' 'Yes, I know AW. I tried them in 1976'. 'Did you really? You'd better go back again and see if they're still as good.'

Who needs Eric?

Wainwright and I had almost come to the end of our meeting. We were discussing how we would realise his Coast to Coast walk. We had talked about possible interviewees, about places it was important to visit, discussed the complicated logistics of filming, and how the whole process would fit into AW and Betty's summer. I thought the meeting had gone well. Ever the accountant, AW was always concerned that everything should be done as efficiently and economically as possible. I had warmed to this theme and chatted about the BBC's finances and how there was never quite enough money to achieve everything I wanted. I mentioned that the very first formal BBC meeting I attended was a pep talk to rally the troops given by the then Managing Director of BBC Radio. The speaker was Ian Trethowan, who went on to hold the top job in the organisation and was later knighted. I remembered only one part of his address and this was a stark warning that the good times – whatever they were – were over.

AW listened to this story and made little comment. Later, as we were preparing to leave for our customary you-know-where lunch – the economy of which should have appealed to Trethowan and his successors – Wainwright told me he had been thinking about our budget and that he had a solution. 'I think we could manage without Eric. He only talks to me and I could do that job just as well. And, whatever you say, he must be quite expensive. I'm sure we could manage without him. Would that help your budget?'

It was a tempting proposition. Only a few months earlier Eric had shown me how easy it was to spend an eye-watering amount on an extended lunch in Glasgow. When I asked how the receipt would pass through the BBC's labyrinthine accounting procedures, Eric succinctly answered, 'say we didn't eat a huge amount – we just kept to the oysters and champagne'. Notwithstanding Eric's extravagance, as I ushered AW back into the vehicle, I suggested this might be one budget cut too far.

Eric trying to orientate himself, blissfully unaware that AW was now happy to film without him!

We gathered on the beach at St Bees on a bracing day when an onshore wind was whipping the waves into white caps. Wainwright was in good spirits, announcing 'This is the beginning of the great adventure...'. He insisted Eric Robson got his boots christened in the Irish Sea. Eric obediently obeyed this command. 'You leave St Bees as a boy, but you finish as a man at Robin Hood's Bay.' Wainwright felt a route was possible almost anywhere across northern England linking the west and east coasts. He told me, 'You could have opened a map of England and stuck two pins in at random with your eyes closed and that would have given you a route from A to B.'

As with all his work, Wainwright demanded that it have a logic and purpose. He describes some of the thinking behind it in the *Personal Notes in Conclusion* that come at the end of *A Coast to Coast Walk*. I found those notes contradictory in many respects, for although he talks of anyone having the ability to plan their own route, he also hints that it will not be as good as this one. He suggests you make your own diversions (for example, travelling via the remote Tan Hill Inn) but immediately says it isn't as good as the line he planned. When we were filming, he spoke to me of a route that would be 'a better way than the Pennine Way with a much more definite start and finish. You can't start any further into the sea here (we were standing at the lighthouse just north of St Bees Head) and you can't go any further when you get to the North Sea, so the beginning and the end are quite definite'.

These are important factors in the enjoyment of any long walk but what especially appealed to AW was the planning of such a route and the challenge of ensuring it followed either rights of way or land where access had traditionally been agreed. This kind of planning requires a wide range of skills: an understanding of the landscape; a sense of how such a journey will be undertaken; where convenient places are located for refreshments, overnight stops or for restocking supplies; and how interest and curiosity will be sustained over nearly 200 miles. It should also require a measure of determination and commitment, but not be a surrogate test of brute force and, perhaps above all, it should inspire a sense of achievement and satisfaction. Wainwright summed it up as follows, 'I think it's great fun to tick off on the map what you've done every day and gradually find yourself getting nearer the objective, and very satisfying when at last you see the North Sea'. And with those thoughts we set off eastwards, although, as AW noted with a smile, at the St Bees lighthouse we were further from our final objective than when we started.

Our filming gave Wainwright more than just an opportunity to retrace the route he had devised some 17 years earlier. It took him into the high places of Lakeland where he once again witnessed how much of this landscape had changed during his lifetime. The snow was still cloaking the high tops when we arrived in my trusty Land Rover at the top of Ennerdale and the Black Sail Youth Hostel. This former shepherd's bothy stands sentinel among some of Lakeland's finest mountains, not least Great Gable and Pillar. Standing with AW looking at this fine, but sombre, panorama I realised he was not simply seeing the mountains as they looked today but was reflecting on the days he came here weekend after weekend whilst working on his original *Guide*. He was speaking of a time when a younger, more active, man had first stood here: 'One of the loneliest places in the district. One of the most beautiful. You're surrounded by mountains. A splendid week's walking from here: different mountain every day. No traffic, no crowds, no litter – wonderful place.' When asked if he had a favourite, he avoided the issue and replied, 'Your favourite mountain is the one you happen to be on at the time'.

Later that day we discovered that, in the four years since our last visit, the Honister slate quarry had closed, a victim to changing economic forces. Another part of traditional Lakeland had vanished and a place that for centuries had echoed to the sound of heavy industry was now silent. I was always fascinated by AW's attitude to conservation in the Lake District. His opposition to the building of reservoirs and the flooding of valleys is well known, but Honister represented something different, an integral part of Lakeland's history and culture. There is little doubt that the quarry was a scar on the landscape (and Wainwright freely admitted that), but he claimed, 'it's such an integral part of Lakeland life that nobody really objects and I certainly don't. Men laboured all their lives on this crag and now it's just like a graveyard'. What he would make of the more recent developments at the site is open to question, although many walkers, including this one, find the cafe a welcome bonus on their journey.

That theme about change affecting the Lakes surfaced again when we arrived at Grasmere and bad weather forced us indoors. Wainwright had a strong romantic streak that is evident in much of what he wrote and to him this village had lost the charm it once possessed. Cars and caravans had spoilt it, so to AW it was, 'frankly a place that I avoid nowadays, except possibly in winter when there's nobody about.' Yet the fells and high tops had lost none of their appeal, although many of them were now beyond his reach. Undoubtedly the most unusual place to stir AW's memory was a stone barn in Grisedale. We had sought shelter there from what seemed like interminable rain accompanied by low cloud. I was staggered to learn that it was not the first time he had found shelter within its four rough walls. He'd been here over 35 years earlier – on Coronation Day, in June 1953. 'It was a public holiday and I came over here, spent the night in this barn without the permission of the farmer and felt a bit apprehensive in case he came along. So I was off at dawn to catch the first bus from Grasmere back to Kendal where I had to be at work by 9.00. When I got back to the office I found that Hillary and Tensing had climbed Everest on the same day, and that rather pricked a bubble for me because I had always had an impossible ambition to be the first man on Everest'.

Wainwright always spoke with great precision about events that had taken place many years earlier, recalling them as if they had happened just a week or two previously and with a significance that the passing years had not diminished. Always a timid trespasser, he had passed the worst part of the night in predictable fashion, 'I was chain smoking. I was afraid to go to sleep in case the farmer came. I had 15 cigarettes that night, one after another until it was light enough to move on'. AW may have been nervous about his night in the barn but he was supremely confident about his *Coast to Coast Walk* and relished sharing it. He was keen that I understood that the crossing of Lakeland, while an obvious highlight, was only part of the journey. Traversing the Pennine watershed, he told me on more than one occasion, was not to be underestimated. Living at that time in one of the most remote communities in these high uplands, I needed little convincing.

As we gathered under the long shadow of Shap Abbey's ruined tower to begin our second week together, I thought about how our filming methods had evolved. At the beginning AW was keen to let the landscape take first place and he was very much in the background. He had been happy to talk on a variety of topics such as industrial history or cultural events to aid an understanding of the landscape, but far less keen to talk about himself or reveal any personal details. I had seen that reticence start to evaporate during our filming in Scotland; now I noticed that he positively enjoyed talking about himself. I also think it was more than just being accustomed to the camera and the film team. It was, as Betty once told me, 'an unexpected bonus for Red'. I realised that the complicated logistics of filming appealed to his need for order. The wonderful reaction that greeted the programmes was the icing on the cake. 'You are now a television star, AW', I told him one lunchtime when he was spotted by an admirer. "Am I? Well, well…' came the reply.

So it was a beaming AW who talked about Shap Abbey and its history. Four years earlier, Eric would have needed to coax this information from him.

Above Keld with Doreen Whitehead. I am sorry I failed to photograph the magnificent food she had cooked for Wainwright and our team. Left to his own devices I suspect AW would have stayed until everything had been eaten - which would have taken the rest of the day and perhaps a bit longer.

When the conversation was over, we set about filming all the images that would be necessary to complete the sequence. Wainwright and Eric needed no prompting for a cigarette break. I would usually be called over and AW would ask, 'Have you got it all Richard?' I began listing the various shots we had and those that we still needed to do. Wainwright became enamoured with the zoom lens on the film camera and its long range. When I was moving around the site with the crew, AW would ask, 'can't you just zoom it, Richard?' and I needed to explain that was no substitute for getting the correct angle and working with the light. While AW had a good eye for a still photograph, his knowledge of filming was informed by the unlikely combination of *Coronation Street* and westerns, both of which were of limited use to the programmes we were trying to make. This lack of understanding was, in fact, a blessing – one which allowed us to capture many informal scenes. At Oddendale, the next stop on our journey eastwards, Eric and AW walked casually towards the hamlet, chatting as they went, while we filmed from a distance. AW was unaware of what was going on, while Eric – the ultimate professional – knew exactly what we were doing.

By now the idea of having a guest or two appear in the programmes was an accepted practice, with AW falsely claiming on camera that it was his choice to invite Tom Clare – then the county archaeologist of Cumbria, later Mayor of Kendal – to join us. When the trio reached Smardale Bridge it was AW who initiated the conversation and who listened attentively when Tom explained the rich and fascinating history of the old road; the so-called giants graves and the ancient settlement of Severals. AW was always fascinated by local history, but nearby Kirkby Stephen had a different type of attraction - the Coast to Coast chip shop. The owner clearly wished for more customers of AW's ilk when, unprompted, he said, 'fish and chips has been my staple diet for 80 years'.

Later, above Keld, we met Doreen Whitehead who published (and kept updated over many years) an accommodation guide for the Coast to Coast walk. In the days before the internet, it provided invaluable help to CtoC-ers looking for a bed. Like AW's guide it was a labour of love that involved detailed research, so Wainwright was keen to express his gratitude for her work – thanks that became all the more heartfelt when he found she had laid on a magnificent spread of sandwiches, pastries, cakes, more cakes and tea for everyone. I said to AW that had he stayed at Doreen's he might never have completed the route – a view with which – reaching out for another sandwich – he readily agreed.

I was amazed to meet Doreen and her husband Ernest 26 years later and discover they still remembered me. They have retired from a hard life of upland farming and now live in the village. Both are in their seventies and Doreen told me she was producing her guide for the last time. Generations of Coast to Coast walkers will thank her for all her hard work and I suspect many of them, like me, will be sad to see her wonderful booklet disappear. The internet may be convenient but it lacks the personal touch and detail of Doreen's work. And, of course, AW did discreetly put some of Doreen's home-cooked ham in his pocket as a treat for his favourite cat. Our couple of hours at East Stonedale Farm ended when, without warning, Wainwright thanked Doreen for both her guide and home cooking. Outside he came up to me and added, 'It's a pity we can't take her with us'.

The Coast to Coast Walk is a wonderful undertaking in its own right but for Wainwright it reflects many of his interests. That was evident as we made our way down Swaledale, his favourite of all the Yorkshire dales. Its rich industrial past is evident wherever you look. That history is firmly imprinted on the landscape and AW observed how the passing of the years had affected what remained of the once dominant lead mining industry. He told me that the roof on Crackpot Hall,

Wainwright and Radio 1

During the filming of A Coast to Coast Walk, AW was intrigued on more than one occasion to discover why the camera crew returned to their car for about ten minutes every morning around 11 o'clock. When he asked me, I told him they were having a short break. 'But they haven't done a lot of work yet', was his gruff reply. Struggling to find an answer, Betty stepped in and said it was a different kind of work. I said something along the lines that camera people needed to 'rest their eye' from time to time, but the truth was more prosaic and something that couldn't be admitted to a man with a strong work ethic.

In common with an estimated eleven million other listeners, they were intently following the latest episode of Simon Bates' Our Tune on Radio 1. Then at the height of its popularity, it was a fixed point in the crew's day. I will never forget the one we heard near Keld, about a woman suffering from cancer whose partner cheated on her – but with another man. If I remember correctly the dog also died. Each day the crew would avidly follow every detail before a quick discussion on its merits – the more depressing the better – and the probability of it being true. As the team exited Richard Ranken's Ford Sierra, I would inform AW that eyes had been rested and it was now back to the task in hand.

once a hill farm, had been intact when he first visited here, now only part of it remained. The detail with which Wainwright researched every aspect of his books had always impressed me. Much of that information could only have been obtained by meticulous and persistent investigation, tracing books long since out of print and talking to local people. Like a conscientious journalist, AW liked to have his information corroborated from more than one source.

Seeing the remains of culverts, hushes, smelt mills, peat houses, mine levels, bridges and abandoned buildings was an obvious source of satisfaction to AW, if a bittersweet one. But his interest did not end there. He was able to place these remains in a wider historical and social context, pointing out that, in its heyday, lead mining had contributed more to the economy and social fabric of this valley than agriculture. Once an all-enveloping activity, employing thousands of people, now 'it has the silence of death about it'. Remembering his own industrial roots, Wainwright was pleased to discover that noted local historians like John Hardy were preserving memories of it for future generations.

The former farmhouse of Crackpot Hall above Keld has deteriorated since Wainwright first drew it, but is still instantly identifiable, standing isolated and due east of Keld. Our filming in Swaledale was a revelation to me, with Wainwright arguably more immersed in the history all around him that the landscape. Perhaps I should not have been surprised, because the industrialisation of this dale was not dissimilar to what took place in his native Lancashire.

The final stage of AW's CtoC shares its route for 40 miles with the Lyke Wake Walk. This route crosses the North York Moors from just north of Osmotherley to south-west of Ravenscar, although there is technically no official line. To add a little spice to the endeavour it is traditional to try to complete it within 24 hours. During our filming we met farmer and walker Bill Cowley. He was in the party that made the first crossing in October 1955 and went on to found a club for those who complete this route. His name is integrally linked with the LWW and like John Hardy in Swaledale, AW was keen to meet him. We learnt that over 100,000 people had completed the route at the time of our filming, all within the 24-hour time stipulation with the legendary Cumbrian fell runner Joss Naylor recording a time of 4 hours and 52 minutes – although that was not the fastest time. Our journey was more leisurely, along the northern scarp of the Cleveland Hills.

Chatting to Bill as we went, we discovered he had done his own route no fewer than 36 times, which comes to an impressive total – just short of 1,500 miles.

Arriving at Robin Hood's Bay was an emotional moment and not simply because we had completed both AW's route and our filming. This was the third series we had made together. Although each one had become progressively more popular and Wainwright was now a more relaxed and accomplished performer in front of the camera, I was wondering how many more programmes we might be able to make. I could see that his eyesight was getting worse, his breathing was becoming more laboured and his ability to walk significant distances compromised. Conversely I also noticed how much the television programmes meant to him, how much he enjoyed the company of the production team and how working on the films had kept him mentally active. After a celebratory drink in the Bay Hotel, for which he paid, AW asked if I was pleased with the filming and indicated that he was sad it was over. I said that only this particular shoot was over. 'Until the next time', I added and received a warm smile in return. Later Betty and I talked about whether we would be able to do another series. We agreed to meet up shortly to talk about it. 'You've given him something special', were her parting words.

There are a few postscripts to the Coast to Coast programmes and AW's route. Richard Ranken's excellent photography and the series as a whole both went on to win awards from the regional branch of the Royal Television Society, which pleased Betty and AW enormously.

I have recently re-walked parts of the Coast to Coast and, even early in the year, was surprised to see just how much its popularity has grown since Wainwright's death. Doreen Whitehead at East Stonedale Farm had told us that even in 1989 it was attracting people from America. While researching this book I stayed at the George Hotel in Orton after a wild, wet day in April when heavy snow alternating with high winds and driving rain made photography impossible. The place was full of CtoC-ers, bringing vital income to this small village. Not having walked 19 or so miles that day I felt somewhat out of place, for this resembled a CtoC convention, with participants from around the world, including Australia and North America. At a time when most rural pubs are either struggling or have closed, there was an almost festival atmosphere here.

I chatted to the owner about the weather, and her clients' destinations. Most were following AW and going west to east, so Kirkby Stephen would be the next stop.

This hotel knows its market, so there is a hearty breakfast with a choice that would put many more expensive places to shame. It is hard to overestimate the impact of AW's *Coast to Coast*: five years ago the George Hotel had closed and the two local B&Bs had to drive their guests to Kirkby Stephen for an evening meal. Now, for ten months of the year, Coast to Coast walkers make up the bulk of their business.

I talked to a father and daughter from the States. He was from Idaho, she from Wisconsin. She undertakes a different walk somewhere in Britain every year and is impressed by the CtoC. Some of the other walkers were well aware of the seriousness of the undertaking, others take it as it comes. Somewhat worryingly, the Australian party asked me how you get rescued...

Yet on one level perhaps the CtoC is a failure, albeit a glorious one. Wainwright wanted to people to use his route as a template, so that they could plan their own. I too have fallen into the trap that awaits almost everyone who follows in Wainwright's footsteps on the CtoC. AW would never hesitate to correct me if he thought I had got something wrong, so I will pass on what he said to me, 'Richard. it's *A* Coast to Coast Walk, not *The* Coast to Coast Walk. As I said in the book, it's just what I did. There's nothing to stop you making your own route'. In the 40 and more years since its publication and in spite of two miles being added to it through access problems, most people think it would be hard to improve on the original. Little wonder, therefore, it is often claimed to be one of the great walks of the world. His template is so good that almost everyone follows it, with perhaps the most rebellious act being to cross from east to west rather than west to east as AW suggested. And a final aphorism to all potential CtoC walkers comes from one of the Australian group: 'What you gain in the beginning, you've got to give back in the end'. They had arrived at the George in terrible weather and the day ahead did not look promising. As we went our separate ways, I thought that these will be the days they remember above all others.

It would be difficult to pluck out a favourite moment during the filming of the CtoC. I would often look at AW and ask if he was happy with progress. A nod, smile or a simple 'yes' was the usual answer. Both of us knew this was a genuine, late life treat for him. My highlight is not from the high fells of Lakeland, the stark relief and penetrating wind of the Pennine watershed or even the rugged, sparse beauty of the North York Moors. Instead it is the lunchtime when we entered the White Swan at

Journey's End at Robin Hood's Bay, although when we filmed in 1987 there no Wainwright's Bar, no plaque and my original photograph shows the hotel was in need of care and attention. AW kindly bought us all a drink but Richard Ranken almost missed out on this treat. Filming the hotel from the beach, he was cut off by the incoming tide and waded back with his precious camera held aloft and to applause from a rapidly gathering crowd.

Danby Wiske. Wainwright had been uncharitable about this pub in his book, but things had changed for the better in the intervening years. Having originally said that all he could obtain here was 'just a bag of crisps', he entered and announced, 'I owe the place an apology'. Opening the visitors book we found a selection of comments from more recent CtoC-ers, including, 'Wainwright, Wainwrong' and 'Correction to Wainwright p116 – 118: Danby Wiske White Swan provides excellent food and accommodation'. Fortuitously two walkers from North Yorkshire had added their comments earlier that morning, noting, 'Wainwright should come here now…'. With that AW got out his pen and wrote. 'He did!!!'

10. The making
of a celebrity

The making of a celebrity. Archetypal Wainwright. Happily sat by the side of the old corpse road above Haweswater, AW has his trusty Three Nuns tobacco and pipe. He is recalling his first visit to what was then a neglected part of Lakeland Today, I am surprised at how busy the (extended) car park is throughout the year.

I found it hard to believe what I saw in the magazine on my desk. A minority interest film about a man in ancient walking boots, old coat and pipe was in the BBC2 programme top 20. The first programme in Wainwright's Coast to Coast series had made it, rated above Ripping Yarns and Ski Sunday and only slightly below a repeat of M*A*S*H. Other programmes higher up the chart were Oranges Are Not The Only Fruit (a drama based on Jeanette Winterson's first novel), The Natural World and Horizon. All had much bigger budgets and production teams many times larger than ours. The orthodox view is clear: television works by realising compelling stories or using articulate and forceful individuals as its presenters and star interviewees. Wainwright was the opposite and we had overturned that perceived wisdom.

There was more good news. Sheridan Morley, writing in *The Times*, had reviewed three out of the four programmes in the series. After the first programme was broadcast he suggested that 'deep in the basement of Television Centre…the BBC maintains a training school for lovable eccentrics…one of the school's senior alumni is Alfred Wainwright'. Morley's first review was witty but somewhat caustic, 'Lest Wainwright appear to be talking to himself all along the way, the BBC have sent him a minder. This is Eric Robson, who is inclined to refer to nearby mountains as "unabashed and unashamed", thereby suggesting a latter-day Wordsworth in uneasy alliance with a boxing promoter.' It didn't matter that Morley had attributed AW's famous description of Haystacks to Eric or that he thought Wainwright was most famous for his offer of a drink upon completion of the Pennine Way. Sheridan Morley was one of the best-known arts figures of the time; a polymath whose work included broadcasting, writing (he was the official biographer of Sir John Gielgud) and as a critic for a number of papers and magazines.

From the late 1980s onwards I witnessed AW's health decline – a decline that accelerated rapidly in his last few years, not helped by his smoking, failure to lose weight and worsening vision. Conversely our journeys became more important to him and any trip which allowed him to be in the presence of his beloved hills was welcome and saw him always at ease with the landscape.

A week later and another review from Morley – this time of programme two from Shap Abbey to Keld and our crossing of the Pennine watershed – and another backhanded compliment to Eric. 'If you must have a friend, he [Wainwright] said, looking sharply at Eric Robson, choose one who is quiet. But the great thing about Robson is that he scarcely ever draws breath at all.' Then came something that all of us, and perhaps especially Eric, should relish: 'I am acquiring a deep devotion to the two of them, especially at their most sharply contrasted. Wainwright is like some great woolly sheepdog, with Robson forever barking terrier-like at his heels'. For a specialist film like Wainwright you would be lucky if one programme was reviewed in the papers, but Morley was intrigued by AW and our very own terrier, Eric.

When our last film was shown – taking the pair to their final destination at Robin Hood's Bay – it was during a week of exceptionally big new stories and the biggest of them all was Nelson Mandela's release from prison in South Africa the previous day. The last thing I expected was another review from a critic who had already written about two of the previous programmes. I was wrong.

'On what promised to be a television night almost entirely devoted to police corruption, with hour-long specials on both *World in Action* and *Panorama* (at least until Nelson Mandela cut a freedom trail through the schedules) some of us had even more important matters to attend to. Over on BBC2 *Wainwright's Coast to Coast Walk* was at last nearing completion.' I had to study what Morley wrote a few times to check I had not misread it. I couldn't have wished for better piece if I had paid for it. Morley was now in contention for being our number one fan. But why? His first review told me that he had done some research on Wainwright, yet it was equally clear that he did not know our previous work. What had made him such a convert? And when the previous night's television reflected events of national and international importance, why was he devoting the whole of his column in *The Times* to a programme made on shoestring budget in a BBC outpost in the north?

Morley was revelling in his writing: '...you may recall, Alfred the great pedestrian and Eric Robson his ceaselessly chattering sidekick set off to plod their way across England from the Irish to the North Sea. At the time, I suggested they were like something out of a minor Pinter play. By the end, they were positively Beckettian...' The hyperbole continued throughout the extended piece, usually at Eric's expense. 'They found a sign about nesting birds being an endangered species, and Wainwright ventured that 3,000 grouse had been shot there during the previous season. "No wonder the buggers keep their heads down," said Robson mournfully, one endangered species recognising another.' I didn't mind how much fun Morley was having reviewing what he described as 'a mysterious series', for the final sentence revealed what our audience felt, 'The terrible thing is that now they have gone, I think I am going to miss them'.

After reading this review I picked up the phone to tell Betty the good news, remembering that in the eight years since the first film had been broadcast, AW had become a cult figure. When I first met him there were no Michael Joseph coffee table books, his works were still published by the *Westmorland Gazette* and I often had to explain who Wainwright was and why his books were work of genuine literary merit, not merely local guidebooks. The vast majority of that change was due to the big audience the films created for AW's work. With hindsight I should not be surprised at the Wainwright 'industry' that has developed, but back in 1982, when we made our first film, the signs had not been promising.

The Wainwright programmes were what, in the industry, is called a 'slow burner'. I had expected the original programme, entitled simply *Wainwright* and presented by David Bean, to generate a lot of publicity. I knew we had a genuine scoop. The key selling point for me was not simply the intricately handwritten books, but the man who had produced them and his life story – the reclusive author who had steadfastly refused to take part in any serious marketing or publicity and whose private nature had only added to the mystery and intrigue of the work. I thought that the closer you looked at this story the more compelling it became. I couldn't imagine anyone else undertaking such a project and moreover doing so without such obvious benefits as having their own transport, or being willing to sacrifice their marriage in order to accomplish the task. Furthermore, AW did this while holding down what I thought was a demanding job as Borough Treasurer. (When I mentioned this to AW one day, he was keen to correct me about the day job. With a broad smile, he said, 'It was easy once I got the hang of it, but I didn't tell anyone that.')

Nonetheless, I was convinced that a programme that contained the first agreed interview with AW would be big news. The area we served was Wainwright's home patch, although, owing to the labyrinthine nature of the BBC's internal politics and vagaries of its transmission system, AW and Betty could not receive the programme in Kendal. Before transmission I took a copy over to them on a VHS cassette and having now unofficially designated myself as BBC Newcastle's outdoor producer, combined that with a night on Haystacks on the way back home. AW concentrated intently on the film, with Betty describing some pictures – usually wide-angled scenic shots – that she thought AW would have difficulty seeing. When it was finished there was a pause, another puff on the pipe. After what seemed a long time, AW finally spoke. Turning to Betty he said, 'Well....?'. Betty answered more quickly, 'I think it's good. Very good. I'm sure people will like it. I do'.

The original 30-minute *Wainwright* was first shown on BBC North East, which included only the northern half of Cumbria, in the autumn of 1982. Afterwards I waited to see what the response might be. In the early 1980s few people, other than politicians and those with a complaint to make, would ring the BBC, especially in

Newcastle. In a time long before the instant commentary of social media, some viewers would be motivated to write in and later in the week letters began to arrive at the BBC in Newcastle. Those we received were all appreciative, but the response was hardly earth-shattering. Put tactfully, the post office did not have to provide extra deliveries to cope with an unprecedented volume of mail.

I was not entirely surprised by this. Wainwright's story was known to many people locally. I was more intrigued to see how the rest of Britain would respond. On Tuesday 3rd May 1983 at 7.05pm the film was shown on BBC2 throughout the UK. The network showing had always been part of a bigger plan, but working in Newcastle had given me a freedom that was not available in London. Although Wainwright was an inspiration to thousands of walkers and his *Guide* was approaching its millionth sale, he was scarcely known to the metropolitan based television executives or the media critics. A lifetime spent avoiding publicity and personal appearances was not helpful when trying to sell a film.

While I was thrilled at having coaxed AW onto the small screen, the television reviewers took more convincing. *The Guardian*, with its strong northern roots and an equally strong reputation for misprints, had the most fulsome preview: *A first-ever interview with the shy author whose Guide to the Lakeland Fells is an indispensable travelling companion for any lover of the Lakes. A. Wainwright talks about the 15 years of painstaking work that went into a definitive and thoughtful study of the landscape he loves.* The *Daily Telegraph* was only slightly less fulsome. They were correct in saying it took 13 years to produce the *Guide* but seemed to think it was just one volume. The *Daily Mail* was brief and merely acknowledged AW's *epic work* in its television listings and that was it. As far as I can discover there was not a single review after the broadcast.

Looking through these papers has been a fascinating experience, especially setting the programmes in the context of contemporary events and the television landscape back then. This was a time when there were just four main channels (and some of us struggled to receive the most recent arrival, Channel 4). Many homes, including mine, did not have a video recorder.

Three years later, in May and June 1986, viewers across Britain were treated to our first series on BBC2 and on the basis that simplicity is best, it was again called *Wainwright* but with the location forming the latter part of the title. *In Limestone Country* was the opening programme and it certainly didn't impress the previewer from *The Sunday Times* who failed to be swayed by either AW or Eric Robson.

'The central pleasure... is hoping that Wainwright will tell reporter Eric Robson to shove off. When he doesn't, interest slips away.' This was a piece I didn't think necessary to bring to either Eric or AW's attention... Fortunately *The Sunday Telegraph* and again the *Daily Telegraph* were more hospitable, with the latter viewing Wainwright as 'a real country character prepared to give only a guarded welcome to any intruder to his solitary world' and Eric would certainly have agreed with their assertion that he 'finds the climb far less strenuous that his efforts to get his shy, reclusive 79-year-old companion to talk about himself'. Even so it seemed as if the media might yet embrace this most unlikely of television stars. In one review the *Daily Mail* described AW as 'being in great form this week'. They made our Haweswater film a 'Pick of the Day'.

But it was Julian Barnes, then working as television critic for *The Observer* and establishing a reputation as an important novelist, who was the first to really understand the films. I had always used one word to describe them – authentic. I didn't want to change AW or to mould him for television. Both, of course, would have been fruitless tasks and I remember an early lesson from our first camera person, John Warwick, about what he described as going with the material, rather than against it. In other words, there was no sense in trying to make Wainwright into something he wasn't, but a lot of sense in celebrating who he was and why his work was important. Why he was, to employ that overused word, unique.

Having seen the first three films of the series, Julian Barnes had clearly understood that. He wrote about 'the most non-cheating travellers seen on the box for a long time...the quiet, elderly, mutton-chopped fell-walker... In the first episode he declared a preference for the solitary, private life: "I wouldn't like to stand up in front of a lot of people and talk". This, of course, is precisely what he is now doing; though admittedly in a most unpulpity fashion, just letting slip a few half-celebratory, half-grumbling asides... Even non-walkers (perhaps especially they) can delight in the views, which are neatly annotated by Wainwright's crusty denunciations of caravan parks and foreign measurements...' And, after mentioning AW's failing eyesight, Barnes finished his review hoping that it would be 'good enough for him to see his own programmes'. I was so delighted that I thought I should take a copy of this over to AW and Betty personally... and get a hill or two in on the way there and back.

With each series the audience and the attention increased, and whatever AW might say in his letters and to his few friends it was clear he was enjoying being in the spotlight. Hugh Herbert was a longstanding *Guardian* stalwart who could turn his hand to many jobs on the paper, including being its television critic, but he also had another life as a writer of fiction. It is, therefore, not surprising that he should latch on to Wainwright's style and he gives, I think, one of the earliest critical assessments of AW's achievement. 'He talks the way he writes, in measured rhythms, with no hurry and perfect clarity. He draws landscape the same way, with all those closely hatched lines that, when they are horizontal seem to shimmer because of the effect of the (television) screen lines, so that a river or a lake suddenly gives the illusions of a fluid life'. A few weeks later I saw the *Daily Mail* and again was impressed by the ingenuity of newspaper hacks. Wainwright was now, somewhat improbably, being compared to one of the biggest television names of the time, the late and hugely popular Russell Harty. The contrast could not have been more stark – Harty was immensely talented, highly articulate and many of his programmes had won awards. His career began as an English and Drama teacher before a move to radio and then television. Our programmes coincided with his heavily promoted series *Grand Tour*. Peter Paterson, himself a distinguished author and editor, had chosen to review both programmes:

> 'An extraordinary touristic contrast in succeeding programmes last night. Wainwright - known cryptically as 'A.W.' – is a stocky bespectacled old gent in a flat hat who throughout his long life has sought out the lonely places in the Lake District and the Scottish Highlands. Just watching him induces a feeling of patriotic well-being.

> 'Russell Harty, on the other hand, despite sharing a Lancastrian birthright, looks more like Frank Sinatra on tour, and is far from restful as he hops around Europe. While Harty revels in it, Wainwright doesn't hold with abroad, with the 'foreign food and alien language'. And it was Wainwright who came up with the best line of the evening, when someone said there was an 'almost Mediterranean light' over a Scottish mountain. 'Is there?' he growled. 'Well, I'll take your word for it'.

The 'someone' in question was Eric and I remember his expression when yet another question had brought forth only a terse, sometimes monosyllabic, reply.

At the head of Gleann Lichd, behind the Five Sisters of Kintail with National Trust for Scotland ranger, Allan Whitfield. This series cemented Wainwright as a television personality with a big and appreciative response from our audience. It helped start a seemingly ever growing trend of outdoor films that has continued unabated.

When we were filming, substantial conversations between Eric and AW were a bonus, but it was the short one-liners that reduced camera person Richard Ranken and I to barely suppressed hysterics. We knew such moments were the filmic equivalent of gold dust. Eric's discomfort was the viewer's gain. Most importantly of all, millions of people had taken Wainwright into their homes and hearts. Naturally, AW complained to me about the arduous nature of being a television star: 'People stop me in the street now, Richard, and I had thirty letters after the first Scotland programme...'. He wanted to pretend this was an unwelcome burden but his face gave the game away. 'You need never have worried about the films', Betty added, but AW was determined to have the last word and pointed his pipe at me. 'It's all his fault.'

11. On home ground

Filming Wainwright's *Coast to Coast Walk* was more difficult than the previous series, but not for the reasons you might expect. Retracing this route was, like his return to Scotland, something he hadn't expected. For the majority of the CtoC filming we did not have the spectacular weather that graced our steps in some parts of Scotland, especially Skye, but that did not seem to matter.

In fact, the late snow flurries that swirled around us in upper Swaledale served only to lend an appropriately sombre atmosphere as we tramped around the remains of the once dominant lead mining industry. While filming those scenes in the high Pennines, I became more concerned for AW's health and well-being. His outdoor clothing – undoubtedly too grand a phrase for old trousers, ancient boots, a jacket dappled with burn marks and a flat cap – was not well suited for standing around when the temperature was in single figures and the wind chill lowered it below freezing. Betty was my touchstone and together we monitored progress. When Betty asked, 'Red, how are you feeling? Are you cold?', the answer was always 'No, I'm fine'. Nonetheless we would ensure he went back to her car for a hot drink and something to eat. If there was a particular viewpoint, valley or structure that AW wanted to visit again, he would be keen to continue whilst I fretted about cold hands and a coat that was rarely properly buttoned. Filming with Wainwright was now far removed from the blustery day on Pen-y-ghent when he made that charismatic appearance in front of the camera. There was no doubt that in the intervening years his health was steadily getting worse. The days needed to be shorter and the walking less arduous.

I mentioned earlier that the CtoC programmes were even more popular than *Wainwright in Scotland* and I was keen to press on with a further series whilst AW was well enough to take part and enjoy the experience. But my timing could not have been worse. The BBC was undergoing one of its periodic upheavals, this one bigger than most and one especially affecting films made outside London. The BBC appointed someone to head up the north region whose sole mission seemed to be to stop all documentary programmes in our building. 'This is year zero', he told the assembled staff without any sense of irony. There was a collective groan.

The result was an enforced delay that, for a few months, significantly soured my relationship with Betty. She and AW, like many people I have worked with, lived an isolated life and I've noticed a characteristic shared by many of them. It is a tendency to believe that the world is set against them. Removed in many ways from the mainstream of contemporary life, they can be prone to introspection. Betty was extremely upset by the news. 'Don't they understand he is getting older?' she asked. 'He won't be here for ever you know'. I totally agreed with her, but such entreaties, and as many other subterfuges as I could muster, were lost on the new regime then in charge. (It was small consolation to discover later that the individual causing me so many problems was later reported to be responsible for a distinguished Head of the BBC's Natural History Unit also throwing in the towel.) To make matters worse I had been making a previously commissioned series looking at the history of mountaineering with Chris Bonington and Betty thought this was at the expense of working with Wainwright. 'Chris Bonington is very important, but so is Red', Betty argued, 'why him and not Red. We might go elsewhere you know'. I tried to explain that the climbing series had external finance, contracts had been signed and could not be cancelled by my new boss. Eventually, after concerted lobbying, we were finally able to proceed. But there had been more frustrating delays in the meantime. Now there was a real urgency to start filming.

Wainwright's Lancashire accent was as strong as ever. It was a beautiful, clear autumn day but rather than looking at the view spread out before us, AW was reaching back through the years, to the time when he first began to escape Blackburn and explore the world beyond the town boundary. He was thinking not simply about the mountains, their characteristic features and even their individual personalities, but about his relationship with them and what they have given him. 'On the hills you'd always the freedom, you weren't disturbed, you could go ahead, get to the top. Great thing always was getting to the top. Which wasn't a bad maxim for life, was it?'

Although much had changed, the house where Wainwright was born at 331 Audley Range is still standing. Today it is suitably adorned with a blue plaque, but when AW walked down the street with the film team we were greeted with only mild curiosity and Britain's most famous guidebook writer went unrecognised.

In spite of my concerns, Wainwright was looking well, smiling and at ease with the camera. With AW, Betty, Eric, myself and the camera team it felt like a family reunion. We were in the afternoon shadow cast by the Jubilee Tower above Darwen, six miles south of Blackburn. This octagonal Victorian monument was an appropriate setting for our filming, having been a favourite destination of the young AW. The building celebrates both Queen Victoria's Diamond Jubilee and local people's access to the moor. This is something they had to fight hard for when the landowner, one Reverend William Arthur Duckworth, tried to close the paths in the 1870s. Normally Wainwright would have wanted to ensure I knew about this history, especially as it concerned the right to roam, but today he was focused on his own background and the forces that shaped his life.

Ostensibly this new series would be loosely based around Wainwright's *Pennine Journey*. He had told me about his eve of war long walk some years earlier and lent me the manuscript long before the work was finally published in 1986. But there was another reason that I chose this as the basis for our new set of films. I thought it could serve as a convenient device to explore more of AW's life. I wanted to begin our re-creation of that journey in AW's home town, Blackburn, rather than 30 miles north-east in Settle, as the younger Wainwright had done in 1938. Long before I met AW, I had been intrigued by his personal journey from the poverty of a terraced house to the Borough Treasurer's office in Kendal. Parallel with this, of course, was another journey, that of a fledgling writer and illustrator to best-selling author and now, a television celebrity.

Even before we received the long-awaited permission for our filming, I had been a regular visitor at Kendal Green, although there was little progress to report. On one of these visits, I began to discuss our future plans. The basic concept was well received, but I needed to enter into potentially more tricky territory: 'I think it would be useful to talk both about the journey we're undertaking and also about you.' 'Do you?' replied AW, followed by a pause. "Really? Would anyone be interested?' Before I could answer, and potentially get myself into deeper water, Betty joined in, 'I think that is an excellent idea, Red. Why don't we think about it?' When we next spoke the idea had taken root. Betty and I were certainly aware that our filming could not continue indefinitely and that, at least in part, explained our joint desire to capture something of a more directly biographical nature whilst we had an opportunity.

With that agreed we set off on our journey, bound for Blackburn. 'I'm looking forward to this', AW said as we arrived at a nondescript hotel just off the town's ring road. Next morning we were out and about revisiting those places that had made a lifelong impression on the young AW. Soon the memories came flooding back. 'None of my pals wanted to come, so I was on my own. But I really enjoyed exploring the area. So that's how I started walking, because nobody would come with me.'

As we began filming we were blessed with warm, dry weather and enjoyed those wonderful northerly views across the moors to Morecambe Bay, the Isle of Man and Cumbria. When AW was a boy, the smog and pollution of industry would have frequently blocked out the hills, so it's little wonder that AW always spoke about his 'escape' from Blackburn. Nevertheless there was an obvious pride for his childhood surroundings. There is that common paradox, which still holds true today, that it often takes an urban landscape to foster a love of the countryside. It is that contrast between a heavily developed environment and its counterpoint – one where natural features still predominate – that make us appreciate the valleys, mountains, rivers, stream and summits all the more intensely.

Wainwright was clear about his early exploits around Blackburn. 'I did a lot of walking because it was the only means of locomotion you could do without a penny in your pocket. It was free, walking was free.' Walking as a means in itself is fine – the Scottish word 'stravaig' captures such undirected wandering perfectly – but many of us like to have an objective in mind. Wainwright often said that his first visit with his cousin to Orrest Head changed his life, but I believe that day occurred many years earlier and we do not, so far as I am aware, know who to thank for it. Sitting just below the Jubilee Tower, AW recalled a gift he received and what it meant to him. 'I started in earnest when somebody gave me a map of Lancashire and that was a revelation to me. I'd heard of places like Burnley and Darwen and Bolton without ever having been to them, but on the map I could see them all and the network of roads that linked them. And there was a canal that I'd seen bits of. You could trace it for miles and this map had all the land over one thousand feet in a darker colour. And all the moors and hills around Blackburn were named. I'd never been able to name them before.' Locating your position on a map is a uniquely satisfying experience. Walking in the hills, it is indispensable. Quite literally, it shows us our place in the world, even if that world is our immediate surroundings. Wainwright shared that view and using a map satisfied his need to know exactly where he was. It also enhanced his success when another summit was reached. 'I found it was more enjoyable climbing up to these hilltops and every objective was the top of a hill. There was usually a cairn there or an ordnance column and to me they were pinnacles of achievement'.

From the Scottish series onwards I thought of our films as a race against time but was surprised that even as AW's health was declining, his determination to make them was undiminished. Our return to his home town gave Wainwright a renewed impetus as he looked back down the years to his youth and the hardships that came with it. We were in Audley Range, the long straight street to the east of the town centre that was AW's childhood home. Walking down the street with Eric and the camera team at a discreet distance on the opposite side, few of the present inhabitants, many of different ethnic backgrounds, gave us a second glance. There is no disguising this street's traditional working class roots, or, as AW said, 'This is *Coronation Street* all over again'.

The undoubted highlight of Wainwright's final journey to Blackburn was his visit to Ewood Park, the home of Blackburn Rovers. There was no sign of the taciturn figure of popular myth as he kept thanking me for arranging this VIP visit. 'And it's all because we are filming?', he asked. When I nodded, he could see that being on television had, after all, some advantages.

And then we were there... on a patch of grass opposite number 331 with its brown stained door. Wainwright needed no prompting. 'There's the house in which I was born, so long ago that it seems to have happened in a different life. The rent I remember was six shillings a week, which very often my mother couldn't afford to pay, so we were usually in arrears. In the kitchen I remember the principle item of furniture was a mangle, where my mother did the washing. And not only her own washing but other peoples'. She'd to do that to keep the family going.' In the 70 and more years since AW's childhood much had changed. The grass mound we were standing on had once been a brickworks, some of the neighbouring houses had also been demolished and although the back-to-back houses were a vivid reminder of a bygone age, in reality more had changed than remained. 'Most things have gone. The school I went to has gone. The chapel's gone. There's very little left that I can recognise.'

One of the very last photographs I took of AW with Eric. Although enjoying himself and looking forward to filming this new series, within a week he would be admitted to hospital. Although he was allowed home for a short period, he was soon re-admitted and died in January 1991.

But there was somewhere that had not changed much over the years. Two miles south-west of Audley Range is Ewood Park, which for over 100 years had been the home of Blackburn Rovers Football Club. More than anywhere else, this was the place AW wanted to visit and there was barely concealed joy when I explained that not only could we go in with the film crew, but that he could fulfil a lifetime's ambition of walking down the players' tunnel and out on to the pitch. 'Can I really?' was his response when I told him the news, 'That will be magnificent. I've always wanted to do that. Did they agree because we're filming?' In the depression years of the 1930s Wainwright had helped form the supporters club and had followed their fortunes ever since. If we were filming on a match day and poor radio reception in the car prevented AW from hearing the result, he was distracted until he could find out the final score. We went into the Rovers ground, not through the turnstiles, but through the directors' entrance and with all the reverence some people reserve for great cathedrals, he said 'We've been invited in and I think, at least, I should remove my cap'.

The indisputable highlight of this visit for Wainwright was that walk out onto the pitch. 'This is an experience I often dreamed about as a lad. This is hallowed ground to me. I think I ought to go down on my knees and kiss this turf.'

Before we reached the centre circle AW was recalling his favourite game, the Cup Final of 1928. There could be no better day when Blackburn Rovers convincingly beat Huddersfield Town 3-1, with Jack Roscamp scoring in both the opening minute and again near the end of the game. The 21-year-old Wainwright was not in the 91,000 crowd at Wembley, but back in Blackburn. 'Radio had just come in then and somebody asked me in to listen to it'. AW was not simply thinking back to that epic final, but analysing how football itself had changed with the passing years, 'The game was better to watch in those days. There used to be five forwards, three half-backs and two full-backs and a goalkeeper. Now they are all sweepers and strikers and things and seem to wander all over the field. It was quite thrilling to see five forwards coming down in a line.' Wainwright walked to the goalmouth, imagining what it would have been like to score. He then stood on the terraces for one last time. All too soon – at least as far as AW was concerned – it was time to leave, but our star was reluctant to go and his final words were both poignant and prophetic, 'Right, let's take a last look round... might never happen again'.

It was a perfect day for AW. Taking photographs of him and Eric inside the Rovers ground, I saw through the viewfinder a man perfectly at ease with himself and the world. Although obviously frail, his health seemed better that I had been expecting. I was also excited because AW's enthusiasm for this new series was clear to everyone. Our star was now a world removed from the man who gave short answers to Eric Robson's questions.

We moved north to Settle to continue our filming at what was the beginning of AW's original *Pennine Journey*. The next morning was not promising. The bright autumnal skies above Blackburn had given way to persistent rain, driven in on a low pressure front. There was an unmistakeable chill in the air, accompanied by driving rain. Everyone could feel the first signs of winter. By lunchtime we had retreated into a cafe and it then became clear that AW was not well. In recent weeks Betty had been sharing her worries about AW's health privately with me, confiding about a number of 'incidents' when she had been with him. Visits to their local GP had become more frequent and more medication had been prescribed. Now she was more anxious than I had ever previously seen her.

Betty was clear that she should take Wainwright home immediately. There was no question that we could continue filming. I watched as she and AW drove off in her little car, turned the corner and vanished into the distance. It was not just our parting in such difficult circumstances that affected me; privately I knew that would be the last time I saw AW.

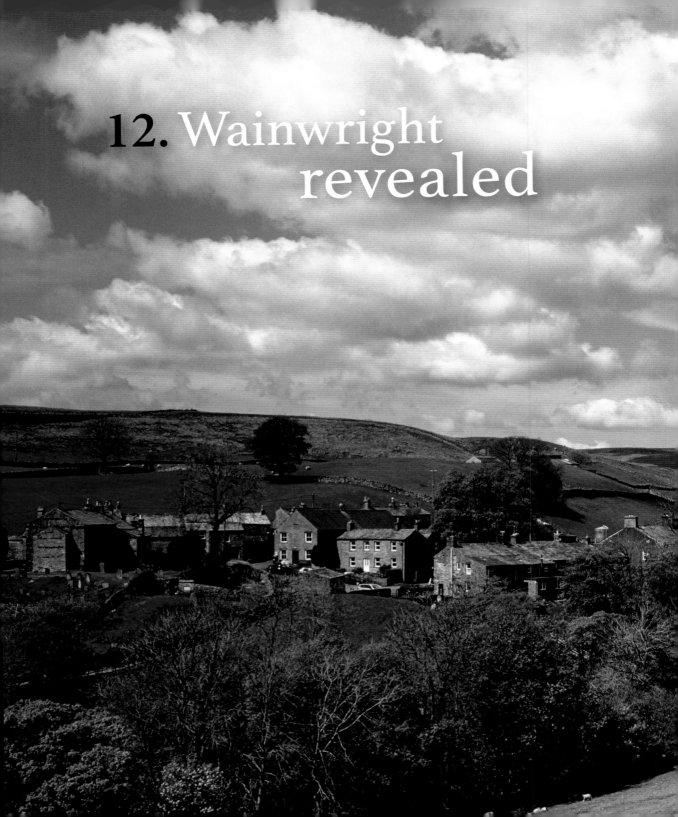

12. Wainwright revealed

By any standards Wainwright was a most unusual person. And that would be putting it mildly. The Wainwright I saw when the cameras were rolling and he was surrounded by the film crew and Eric was different from the days we spent by ourselves. I observed a man at ease with himself, but also one who could be stubborn, difficult and anxious. So who was Wainwright?

To answer that we need to look beyond the image he wanted to portray in those two curious books *Fellwanderer* and *Ex-Fellwanderer*. For the man who was, by his own admission, a backroom boy who valued his privacy, he could not have chosen a worse vehicle than the *Guide* with which to remain anonymous. It should have been obvious that once the first volume was published, his readers would want to know more about the author. After all, no one had previously attempted a work on this scale devoted to Lakeland.

The actual filming was the last part of a long process. Normally you go out on location with a detailed schedule, listing what you hope to achieve during the day and a timeframe for achieving this. I quickly discovered this would not work with Wainwright. It seemed clear that AW gained a great deal of pleasure from our films. Their success was entirely unexpected and Wainwright became a surprise hit with millions of viewers – most of whom would never stride out across Lakeland, tackle the boggy uplands of the Pennine Way or have the time or energy to walk from one side of England to the other. I am also sceptical about thinking of AW as a reluctant convert to television. You only have to look at his first television appearance, interviewed by David Bean, to see that he is relishing every minute. It is a set piece

At home in his adopted home town of Kendal. AW was happy to show us around here and we spent a busy afternoon exploring the alleyways known as 'yards' which, even today and often much altered, form an important part of this community and its history.

that he had planned in exact detail and then executed with great aplomb. But there was another aspect of Wainwright's character that was less easy to understand. However good any day's filming – and many were excellent – the next morning I faced the challenge of trying to renegotiate my relationship with him entirely from scratch.

We may have returned the previous evening delighted by a successful day – the weather kind; the crew pleased with the photography and sound; Eric happy with his interviews and, most importantly of all, AW in good spirits. All this would count for little the next morning. The momentum we had built up would be lost and I felt we would be starting from the beginning again. Initially I found this disconcerting, wondering what I might have said or done to produce such a change. Later I came to realise that this was something deeply embedded within AW. Often it was hidden below the surface, sometimes it was more obvious.

Each day felt as if the trust and mutual respect we had for each other had simply vanished overnight. Betty was a great help in re-establishing this relationship, mainly through telling AW that we were all trying to do our best and that we all shared the same goals and objectives. She would say how supportive and committed the team were and that he should trust us and play his part in trying to ensure the filming would be successful. She would say to me, 'I've had a word with Red. Let's see what happens'.

AW seemed happiest when the filming day fitted his predetermined template with fixed points that he could use like anchors. Once we had agreed a schedule for the week, he found alterations hard to accept, even when caused by changing weather conditions. I lost count of the times Betty would say quietly but firmly, 'Red, I think Richard knows what he's doing. He's trying for the best'.

With the benefit of hindsight, I also misjudged the situation. We spent so much time together without the film crew and Eric and those days were always memorable. We had a mutual love of and respect for wild places – whether big panoramic landscapes or the close up details of becks, tarns, corries, summit ridges and natural rock sculptures. Such sights, and a hundred other things besides, had shaped our lives. So when we met the first thing we always did was to exchange anecdotes – I might talk to AW about the previous night I'd camped on Haystacks on the way over to Kendal. His face would widen when I told him my tent weighed less than three pounds – in the 1980s at the cutting edge of technology – had two tiny poles and was little more than a bivouac sack, necessitating crawling in and out. My stove was equally a miracle of innovation, initially developed for big wall climbing. AW would listen and then, with a puff on his pipe, announce, 'That may be fine for you... but it's not for me. I wouldn't like that at all. Did you get any sleep?'

He was a man who could be good company, someone I could talk to about things that mattered. Someone who understood the importance and beauty contained in OS maps and could be accurate in their use. And, as I often said to his obvious bemusement, I enjoyed using a compass. Yet this blinded me to other, arguably more important aspects of Wainwright's personality. There was a part of AW that allowed him to function as part of a group when necessary. We can see this in the cartoons and drawings he circulated around the Blackburn office, or the co-founding of the Blackburn Rovers supporters club. Later he ran an efficient and effective Treasurer's department in Kendal. But no one would, I think, ever describe Wainwright as a social animal. And, of course, the evidence for him being a solitary being who preferred his own company is well documented. So when he remembers exploring the hills outside Blackburn by himself because, 'none of my pals would come with me...', we should also note that he didn't especially miss their company and was content to undertake such journeys on his own. The seven-volume *Guide* was a lone undertaking. Crucially, I came to realise that AW was not solitary simply by choice. There were other, deep seated and powerful factors at work.

The first time I met Wainwright I was immediately struck by his need for order. In describing how he wanted David Bean to conduct the interview and John Warwick to film it, the instructions went beyond a simple desire to be in control. I thought then how much he needed this secure framework in order to function – something, of course, he found in his accountancy career. On that first day I felt this was something rooted deep within his psyche and not the worries of an insecure or nervous individual facing the camera for the first time. Having sent a message that we were to visit him, he was charming – quite the opposite of the taciturn character of popular myth.

As our friendship developed, I realised that what might best be called an obsessive need for order permeated everything he did, from the most trivial event to the major filming sequences. I was also surprised by the way he treated people like Andrew Nichol, the Publishing Manager at the *Westmorland Gazette*. Andrew was diligent, attentive and had AW's best interests at heart, yet Wainwright was often unduly critical of his efforts. It was not something I wanted to hear, especially as Andrew had been a great ally in originally getting the films made. What I saw time and again was a lack of empathy towards Andrew and a failure to connect with him on a human level. Nor was Andrew the only one to be treated in this way. At first I wondered if AW was simply being curmudgeonly: letting familiarity see someone's supposed faults rather than their attributes. I wondered if he had been affected by years of solitary working on his *Guide* and that unsuccessful first marriage. I soon began to change my mind.

I discovered a compulsive rigidity in all aspects of AW's life. It extended from the way he planned his books, to visiting the same cafe and eating the same food every Saturday night when Keswick was his base for exploration. He told me about reading every western book that was held in Kendal library – not detective fiction, or adventure or historical narratives, just westerns. He talked about the jungle of a garden when he moved into his new house in Kendal Green. Most people would set about taming it as and when they got the time. Wainwright was different: in *Ex-Fellwanderer* he recalls that having had a five-year plan for the work (which he refers to somewhat grandly as a 'programme'), he managed to complete it in two by working in the evenings – summer and winter alike. What he also told me was even more bizarre. He had electric lights strung around the garden to provide illumination and sometimes laid himself out on the ground so he could roll from one side to the other to work in a more efficient way. One wonders what the neighbours thought of this! Although, as he later explained, the plan did not really work because the garden became a jungle again as work on the *Guide* progressed and took up all his spare time.

The need for an all-enveloping order can be seen throughout AW's work. Whether he was showing me his half-inch Bartholomew maps of Scotland, or those he used while working on the Pennine Way, I found they were not simply annotated, as you would expect, but followed a set pattern, even down to the coloured inks he used. Of course, the need for order is nowhere more clearly seen than in the *Guide*. Today we take its structure for granted, but step back a little and it is possible to view it differently. Anyone other than Wainwright tackling such a project would take a different approach. Another author would select perhaps 25 or 50 summits and would probably choose the obvious line of ascent, with perhaps a subsidiary one mentioned. AW was different; he developed an overall template for both the whole work and for each individual fell. No mountain is so important, for example, that it would merit a double-page illustration at the start of the chapter.

Wainwright had his plan and he stuck to it with determination. The result is that readers can continue their exploration of Haystacks in a non-linear way, following the landscape in no fewer than six adjoining chapters in *The Western Fells* and, depending where your route goes, into another of the books. This makes Wainwright's work more comprehensive than any attempted previously, but, as I said at the beginning, it can make the books difficult to use and, perhaps, more suited to being read at home than outdoors. This is not meant as a criticism, but does, I believe, tell us something about the author.

Looked at another way, you might ask why anyone would want to work in that way. How many authors would devote a chapter, so near the start of a book, to Arthur's Pike in *The Far Eastern Fells*, especially when, apart from the crags that overlook Ullswater, 'there is little to excite'? The ridge route to neighbouring Loadpot Hill fares little better and is dismissed as 'dull' and the landscape a 'nightmare' when enveloped in mist.

Even when his eyesight was failing, Wainwright always took a map with him. Here, at the Spittal of Glenmuick, he is showing Eric his old Bartholomew's map and explaining how he planned his annual journeys to Scotland.

Wainwright's need for order, patterning, categorisation and predictability can be seen in many other ways. It appears not only in expected places like his lists of best fells, summits, places to be (apart from on a summit) and finest ridge walks, but elsewhere too. There is the best square mile of Lakeland, around Castle Crag in Borrowdale. Even if we accept AW's argument that this is the 'loveliest square mile', although it contains no mountain or lake, I find it fascinating that he felt the need to label it in this way.

There is also the more philosophical question of what compelled AW to produce not simply the *Guide* but over 50 other works. While it might be argued that the *Guide* was an antidote to his unhappy first marriage to Ruth, what about the subsequent works in the years when Betty was his constant companion, soulmate, and surrogate manager?

When we were filming our second programme, around Haweswater and the drowned village of Mardale, AW spoke about the genesis of his now famous *Guide*. While working on the first volume, *The Eastern Fells,* he had devised a template for the whole work. 'I didn't want to send it to a publisher because having done everything in handwriting, I wanted everything to be reproduced exactly as I'd done it. I didn't want printers changing the layout, and putting things on the next page, I wanted every page to be as I'd done it. So I thought, well the only thing to do is to publish it myself.' The remainder of this story is well known. So well known in fact, that we probably do not fully appreciate its significance. In 1955, when *The Eastern Fells* was published, all books with hardly any exceptions would be typeset by printers; few contained many illustrations or drawings and photographs would often appear as grouped pages separate from the printed matter.

The idea of producing a book that was handwritten was extremely rare. Wainwright's determination to publish the book in this way – even though he did not have the funds to finance it – points to someone who was not only unusually determined, but could not cope with the prospect of his work being altered in any way. Most authors put their effort into the editorial content and leave the layout, design etc to the skills of others. Even late in his life, when books published by Michael Joseph were typeset, Wainwright demanded to be responsible for the layout and fiercely argued the point with his editor, Jenny Dereham. She was a highly experienced publisher who was not used to being treated in this way. (If you are unfamiliar with this story it is well documented by Hunter Davies in both *Wainwright – the Biography* and *The Wainwright Letters*.)

During the time I was with Wainwright and in the years that have followed, I have thought about his attitude and psychological make-up, in particular the way he behaved with other people, and I came to the view that this was not deliberate or the action of someone who wished to be awkward. Neither was it, in spite of what I have just stated, the action of an individual who wished to be *deliberately* controlling. That Wainwright behaved in the way he did was, I concluded, an involuntary act. That has led me to consider if today he might be placed on the autism spectrum or even diagnosed with Asperger syndrome. Of course, there is no way of knowing this for certain and any diagnosis should have input from a number of medical specialists.

In any event, autism is a spectrum condition and people can present in different ways. Today it is still vigorously debated but I think it is generally agreed that

Asperger syndrome affects how people with it perceive the world and also how they interact with others. Today it is accepted that around 700,000 people in the UK are living with some form of autism, although I have known people where the condition has gone undetected for many years. These people have managed to get through daily life by one means or another until, sometimes helped by others, they have sought advice which may include both medication and counselling. Recalling those people I see many traits in common with Wainwright.

I believe AW may have been, in the terminology currently used, 'on the spectrum'. Certainly there are some indicators that would apply to him, including how an individual relates to and understands other people together with persistent difficulties around social communication and interaction. Likewise, there are restricted patterns of behaviour that show elements of repetition. Those placed on the spectrum usually face challenges especially with social skills, flexible behaviour, empathy and communication. They may appear insensitive and find it hard to form friendships. Significantly, such people often find the need for a daily routine (which can include eating the same food); they can be uncomfortable with the notion of change and may have highly focused interests. It is, I would suggest, wrong to think of Asperger syndrome as a mental illness; more correctly it is a developmental disorder.

With this in mind, it is useful to look again at one of Wainwright's more curious works, *Ex-Fellwanderer*. AW showed me the manuscript of this prior to its publication in January 1987. Notwithstanding the similarity of its title, it is a vastly different work from *Fellwanderer*, published some 20 years previously. This earlier book is, in AW's description, 'the story behind the guidebooks'. It was written at a time when many people knew little about the author but admiration for his books was quickly growing. *Ex-Fellwanderer* is an altogether darker work but one that is more revealing about Wainwright. Betty was keen to get my view on it. She had reservations about many of the more forthright passages and there had clearly been much discussion about them. I remember Betty telling me that she hoped AW might tone some of them down. Ultimately she was unsuccessful. So what clues can we glean from this book?

In *Ex-Fellwanderer* Wainwright talks about retreating from friends in the office, preferring to be solitary and has a 'fetish' which is 'almost an obsession', for neat ledgers. When he recalls first visiting the Lakes or moving to Kendal there is no suggestion these were joint decisions made with his then wife Ruth. (In fact, Hunter Davies mentions walking holidays in 1940 and thereafter where AW took his young son Peter, but not his wife.

When he visited Animal Rescue, Cumbria at Kapellan north-east of Kendal, after checking on the cats and dogs waiting to be re-homed, AW would often rest in a caravan in the grounds. Here he seemed at peace and quietly proud of what the royalties from his books and television programmes had helped to achieve.

A year later Ruth temporarily left the marital home, taking Peter with her.) When Wainwright retired from the Borough Treasurer's office in Kendal, Ruth left for good. 'I was not greatly concerned' is AW's terse comment. However, when it comes to cruelty to animals he is extremely concerned. Many might share those views, but fewer, I would suggest, would agree with his solution. So exercised is Wainwright that he would wish humans to be subject to the same treatment he argues is inflicted on animals. It is not only what Wainwright says – for example, suggesting that 'murderers and terrorists and rapists and muggers' be substituted for animals in medical experiments – but the ferocity with which he expresses these views.

When I began to question if Wainwright might have been on the spectrum, I also thought of my own interactions with such people, particularly those I knew or have taught. In many cases I was only aware of their situation when they were professionally diagnosed. Then there are the personal experiences that such people report. When someone told me they had no interest in politics or the wider world, there is an immediate echo of Wainwright's writing, almost at the end of *Ex-Fellwanderer*, 'I am a detached observer…keeping everybody and everything at an arm's length. I am unperturbed by wars and famines and have no time at all for party politics'.

There has been recent research into how people on the spectrum may have more compassion for animals than for humans. This appears to be supported by much personal testimony. Animals have the ability to be unconditionally affectionate and, it could be argued, their behaviour is simple and predictable. Their emotional demands are not great and communication with them is relatively straightforward. Those on the spectrum have spoken of a special affinity with animals that they do not have with fellow humans, with one reporting that they could not love their child more than they did their pet.

Returning specifically to Wainwright, we might speculate that the production of his *Guide* was more important that rescuing his marriage. And devoted as he undoubtedly was to Betty, he was not prepared to alter any of the more contentious passages in *Ex-Fellwanderer*. Does this matter? I think it does, for a number of reasons. When I saw – as I did on many occasions – how he could treat people with a lack of empathy, I did not consider this to be deliberate. It was not the result of being awkward or socially deviant. I think it can also help explain, and perhaps it is the only coherent reason for, the comprehensive and unique nature of his epic *Guide* and why it is highly unlikely that anyone will ever attempt this kind of work again.

It underpinned his behaviour when we were filming, right from our first location day on Pen-y-ghent when his improbable scenario was possibly the only way he could make sense of the process. I fact when I suggested alternatives it was clear to me that AW could not fully understand them. He had worked through a certain scenario and could not contemplate any other. The thought of changing it was a concept he could not process. It also clarifies why, when we finally realised Wainwright's dream of visiting Cape Wrath, he simply said, 'I'm glad I've seen it'. AW was not being diffident or awkward. For him, this was a literal truth. He'd always wanted to see it and now he had. It was as simple as that. There are many similar incidents. Lucy Jolly, our Production Assistant on the CtoC, reminds me of Wainwright asking our camera person, Richard Ranken, if he had to buy and pay for the film we used. This caused much amusement, but for AW it was a serious question and he didn't really understand why it might be funny.

What I believe the *Guide* gave him were substitute friendships from the many people who wrote to him, often c/o the *Westmorland Gazette*. Until Betty came along, these were friends he failed to find in everyday life. Friends that, in spite of the increasing letters he received, made few emotional demands on him, but who he knew were there. He could appreciate their comments, while not having the stress of a face to face relationship. Indeed, when you read both of Hunter Davies' books, and follow the story of AW's courting of Betty and his apparent ambivalence towards her American suitor Ade Meyer, you might conclude that he had little understanding about the complexity of such relationships.

I have tried to be cautious in reaching the above view. What has surprised me is talking to medical professionals who are also keen walkers and are knowledgeable about Wainwright's work. With all the caveats that apply, most obviously that it is no longer possible to discuss this with AW, their answer has been that such a conclusion seems consistent with what we know about him and his work.

There is one final comment I would make. If Wainwright was not, to take the opposite view, someone who was on the spectrum, we are left with the unpalatable conclusion that here was a man who was often wilfully uncooperative, rude and curmudgeonly. That is not the Wainwright I knew.

The Reluctant Foodie

It was rare that the filming overran. I was conscious of AW's age, his frailty and also his diabetes — which had recently been diagnosed. One day, though, we were running late. Filming in a remote part of western Scotland had gone well, but it had taken longer than expected and we had wanted to make the most of good weather, especially as it was forecast to change. With the prospect of a good hour's drive back to the hotel, I suggested that we should stop for something to eat on the way. Betty thought this a good plan but when we stopped at the only restaurant in many miles, my heart sank.

The place had been given a makeover and the proprietors had clearly thought it a good idea to introduce the notion of French-style cuisine. The menu was ornately produced with a typeface imitating florid handwriting. Even with good eyesight, it was difficult to understand, so Eric offered to read it aloud. I could see AW getting more disconcerted and looking worried. He had no idea what most of the items were and no real desire to find out. Finally Eric was finished. 'What was that you said... goujons of plaice and something else I didn't understand', asked Wainwright, picking up on the only word in the description he understood. Eric rose to the moment with aplomb, 'If we miss out the pretence, it's basically fish and chips'. 'Oh', came the instant reply, 'well why don't they call it that then?'

A meal fit for kings and also guidebooks writers with very strong culinary preferences!

13. Wainwright's legacy – and a final goodbye

Wainwright's legacy – and a final goodbye. *Haystacks – a summit that, with the adjacent Innominate Tarn, will now always be associated with Wainwright and especially his seven volume Guide. Perhaps there is no finer place to appreciate his achievement - the passion of his writing; the precision of his drawings and his love of landscape throughout every season. It is hard to envisage anyone will ever have as detailed an understanding of Lakeland as AW. More improbable still is that they will be able to express it so eloquently and with such care.*

It is over 25 years since Wainwright died in January 1991, yet interest in the man and his work is little diminished. At the time of writing an original framed and signed drawing of Ennerdale is being offered for almost £800; a first edition of one of his many books of drawings will cost around £100 and a coveted first and signed edition of one of the seven volumes that comprise the *Pictorial Guide to the Lakeland Fells* is around £600. The original, limited edition of *Westmorland Heritage* is over the £1,000 mark and if you are looking for what some have called the most scarce book – *Wainwright in Lakeland* by AW and Mary Burkett, published by Abbot Hall Art Gallery – the first signed edition has been offered at over £2,000.

When people ask me about Wainwright, I talk about the originality of his *Guide*. I ask them to try to imagine what it would be like to document almost every square foot of the Lakeland fells, in words, images and wonderfully innovative maps and diagrams. I explain that he wanted to show virtually every practical route up to the summits. I then ask them to consider the sheer scale of the work: an author determined to set his *Guide* in the wider context of Lakeland's social, economic, cultural and political history and its geographical and geological influences.

There are many examples of where Wainwright has changed our attitudes to the fells, perhaps most notably in bringing our attention to lesser visited tops or once neglected valleys. It has been argued that, in doing this, he has helped spread our footprints more evenly throughout Lakeland. Conversely, his clear preferences for the best routes of ascent have funnelled many people into following them without considering the alternatives. Wainwright is an excellent guide, but like all guides, he is not infallible. Incidentally, he was also not above changing his mind. I recall him saying I should film around Sunbiggin Tarn, east of Orton, on his CtoC route. It was, he said, 'A beautiful and remote spot. It's full of atmosphere. You should go there'. I was surprised as this is at odds with his description in his book, where he wrote of it as, 'little more than a large reedy pond in the middle of a morass'. I read this out to him and said that was his previous view. 'Did I say that? It's a beautiful spot', came the reply, 'Anyway Betty likes it. You'll like it too'.

Wainwright always claimed that his Lakeland books were written so that in old age he could be reminded of his expeditions in the fells, but this is nowhere near the whole truth. We know that he produced embryonic mock-up 'books' from an early age and that he actively sought to publish his *Guide*. In any event, it would be rare that anyone would so carefully plan a series of books in such detail entirely for their own amusement.

So what is Wainwright's legacy? It is, I believe, not one simple accomplishment. What he did in the seven volumes that constitute his *Pictorial Guide to the Lakeland Fells* was to re-invent the traditional guidebook in a number of ways. It is rare, for example, to see a work where the illustrations are as important as the text. AW was a fine draughtsman, especially in his portrayal of the hills, valleys, stream and becks that make up the Lake District. These drawings are especially important in being penned by someone whose life was dominated by wild places. They contain detail vital to appreciating their characteristic features. His work, which is almost photo-realistic in nature, is at its best, I think, on these natural features capturing the sweep of a landscape with the deft use of perspective that draws the eye to what matters most. Not all his illustrations were as successful: his cartoon-like depiction of people and more often cars (which he had no interest in other than as a way of getting him to a chosen location), does not sit well within the broader framework of the page.

AW also liked his lists. Within his books there are many examples of this preoccupation: best summits, best lines of ascent etc. It is this need to categorise that puts him firmly in the tradition of early writers. In fact, it could be argued that most guidebooks have this list mentality at their heart. Looking at any chapter in the *Guide* will easily illustrate this. For those who are inclined to slavishly follow a guidebook writer, there is the potential problem, as Parsons mentions in *Worth the Detour*, that you fail to see the place for yourself and don't experience it with fresh eyes.

In the shadow of Ben Hope, in the far north of Scotland. AW was always concerned that we were capturing on film the key aspects of a particular landscape. 'Are you sure you have it all, Richard', was a frequent refrain.

With each successive book Wainwright also became more confident in expressing his opinions. Sometimes these may appear idiosyncratic, but views change over time and some of what he wrote now belongs to a previous age. On a more positive note, Wainwright also helped shape public taste, not least through an appreciation for, and understanding of, our upland landscape. He educated successive generations to appreciate the totality of our landscape and not just the obvious summits of Scafell Pike, Great Gable, Helvellyn and the like.

As an aside, it's also important to see Wainwright's achievement in terms of his original books, not the revised or walkers' editions. While the latter have been executed as sensitively as possible in some respects, we cannot now be sure what AW wrote and what has been added later. In some cases, a whole page has mysteriously vanished. AW was the first to say that there is no end to the act of revision by the author. He told me that, once started, this process could carry on *ad infinitum*.

Essentially, I have always considered his *Guide* to be a literary masterpiece. I do not think that is an exaggerated claim. If that definition is correct – and I believe a strong case can be made for it – then it has significant implications. We do not modernise a painting by Constable or Turner by adding new brushstrokes to reflect a changed landscape. So why should we tinker with a work of genuine literary merit and importance?

When it became common knowledge that AW's eyesight was failing, there was no shortage of people offering to help with his books. Such offers were undoubtedly well intentioned and Wainwright would show me letters which contained examples of their work. On every occasion, without exception, Wainwright was absolutely clear to me that he did not wish to see his books revised by others. He did say 'not in my lifetime' to placate some of those who wrote, but told me this was a way of hopefully stalling the issue. More than once and over a considerable period of time, he told me that the books should be left exactly as he had written them.

Today there is a temptation among some of his most fervent followers, to see AW as akin to being a god of the hills – someone whose pronouncements are always correct and whose recommended routes are to be followed religiously step by step. Obvious as it may seem, we should ask some simple questions. 'What was AW's relationship to the Lakeland landscape?', 'How would we describe his core values and beliefs?' and 'How, some 50 and more years after the first volume of the *Guide* was published, should we assess his contribution to the genre of guidebook writing?' The questions may be straightforward, but the answers are more complicated. AW's contribution is more important and far-reaching than many recognise. Indeed, it is only in recent years that his works have received any critical study. For books that have sold well over a million copies this is a startling omission.

Wainwright once asked me why I had made our original film and what had drawn me to his works. The answer was simple: I just said, 'Because I believe they are the best books to have been written about Lakeland.' 'Do you?' he replied, 'do you really?' And that is why, over 60 years after the publication of the first volume, Wainwright is still the best guide to this spectacular part of England.

Acknowledgements

Thank you... to everyone who contributed so much to all the Wainwright films, especially two exceptional camera people, Richard Ranken and the late John Warwick; editors Ian Sutherland and Derek Inglis; the production team of Fiona Clark, Lucy Jolly, Mark Murray and Julie Scott. I am pleased to report that all have flourished thereafter. In front of camera I want to remember the late David Bean. A heartfelt thanks and much more besides to my old friend Eric Robson - a wonderful presenter, raconteur and adopted Cumbrian. I learnt much from him and some of it is even related to filmmaking... Without John Mapplebeck, for many years BBC Newcastle's legendary Features Editor, there would have been no Wainwright films. His great gift was a visionary approach to documentary production, although AW would not have approved of his accounting procedures which allowed me the freedom to roam far and wide. John's largesse was made possible by the exceptional financial wizardry of Anna Gosselin.

Thanks too to a friend of twenty years and more, outdoors writer and television presenter, Cameron McNeish. A friendship forged on the summit of Mount Elbrus is one set in fire and ice. Another McNeish (they get everywhere), Gregor has, as ever, expertly designed the book you are holding and has overseen its production. Roger Smith deserves a special vote of thanks. Not only did he proof read and index this book, but he provided a much wider and much valued contribution based on his expert knowledge of the outdoors.

Others who have been helpful in formulating my view on AW include my long-term Professorial friend and collaborator, Fred Robinson, together with the many Wainwright enthusiasts I've spoken to as they made their way to various summits or along the Coast to Coast route. It might now be clear why the grey-haired man with the medium format film camera was asking so many questions... Likewise many thanks to those who had the privilege of knowing AW and members of his family.

The staff of the National Library of Scotland are not only expert and efficient but also unfailingly friendly. This institution is nothing less than a national treasure.

Thanks to all the long-suffering members of my family. Sara and James have their own successful careers and would not want their future prospects damaged by a public admission that I am their father. Not so lucky is Meg, a research historian turned award-winning filmmaker, who has been looking after base camp for over 40 years.

We weren't exactly Hollywood! Filming around Kendal Castle for the final programme in our first series. From left to right: Betty Wainwright; Production Assistant, Julie Scott; camera assistant, Paul Otter (loading new film in a light proof bag); camera, John Warwick and associate producer and film editor, Ian Sutherland.

When I met her, she had recently returned from crossing Norway's Hardangervidda mountains in the first snows of winter. Surviving for many days on two or three chocolate bars and overnighting outside with just a sleeping bag, she has taught me the most important lesson of all. There is never an excuse for saying something is impossible and, now officially an elder citizen, she still maintains an undiminished love of wild places.

This book was begun during an overnight camp on the summit of Haystacks and finished while tramping the Northern Fells. I have tried to accurately reflect the comments of those I have spoken to but any interpretation or errors are mine alone. Finally, I wish it were still possible to thank AW and Betty - what wonderful times and great journeys we had together, but you know that, don't you?

Further reading

Not all of Wainwright's books are still in print, but those that remain available are published by Frances Lincoln. Most can also be obtained secondhand.

For anyone discovering AW for the first time, I would suggest:

A Pictorial Guide to the Lakeland Fells (7 volumes)

Pennine Way Companion

A Coast to Coast Walk

My own view is that the original, unrevised editions are the most useful, but if you intend following any route, they should be checked against current Ordnance Survey maps, especially the 1:25,000 Explorer series.

Also of interest are:

Fellwanderer (which AW called, 'The story behind the guidebooks')

Ex-Fellwanderer (published to commemorate his 80th birthday)

A Pennine Journey (the story of his long walk in 1938)

Walks in Limestone Country

Walks in the Howgill Fells

Frances Lincoln also publish two of Hunter Davies' books:

Wainwright – The Biography

The Wainwright Letters

The Wainwright Society do much important work to ensure AW's legacy continues for future generations and also produce an excellent magazine and other works. Details are at: www.wainwright.org.uk

For anyone wishing to discover more about the guidebook tradition I can recommend *Worth the Detour* by Nicholas T Parsons (Sutton Publishing).

In spite of the wind and rain and a worry about how we would get back, this was a day I can never forget. This is the final photograph I took that day on Haystacks.: AW alone with his memories, after we had finished filming.

Index

Note: Page references in *italic type* refer to illustrations. Reference titles in *italic* are for books or other publications.